Grenada:

THE STRUGGLE AGAINST DESTABILIZATION

Chris Searle is an English writer, teacher and poet who worked for two years as a teacher-educator in Grenada. He has written such works as *The Forsaken Lover: White Words and Black People*, which won the Martin Luther King Award in 1972, *Classrooms of Resistance* (1975), *The World in a Classroom* (1977), a collection of short stories *The Black Man of Shadwell* (1976) and *We're Building the New School!* (1981) about a secondary school in Mozambique. His poems are included in *Mainland* (1974), *Red Earth* (1980) and *Common Ground* (1983). *Sunflower of Hope* (1982) is his collection of translated poems of the Mozambican Revolution.

He is also the author of *Words Unchained: Language and Revolution in Grenada* to be published by Zed Press in 1984.

This book was written and compiled in the months before the tragic events of 19th October 1983, and the deaths of Maurice Bishop, Unison Whiteman, Jacqueline Creft, Norris Bain, Fitzroy Bain and Vincent Noel, amongst others.

History will reveal the part played in those events by the concealed dagger of imperialism. The voices of those killed shout out through the pages that follow, echoing the struggling history of the Caribbean people.

C.S.
22nd October 1983

Grenada:

THE STRUGGLE AGAINST DESTABILIZATION

by Chris Searle

including an interview with MAURICE BISHOP, Prime Minister of Grenada and Leader of the Grenada Revolution

Our people take a stand
Not one blade of grass, we say
Not one grain of sand
Shall be taken from our land
Kojo de Riggs

Writers and Readers Publishing Cooperative Society Ltd.
144 Camden High Street, London NW1 0NE England

Published by
Writers and Readers Publishing Cooperative Society Ltd.

Cover Design Chris Hyde

Typeset by Inforum Ltd, Portsmouth
Printed by H & T Lithographic Ltd, London

ISBN Paper 0 86316 059 X

CONTENTS

ILLUSTRATIONS

ACKNOWLEDGEMENTS

In particular I would like to thank the journalists and workers of *The Free West Indian*, Grenada's national newspaper, for it has often been an important source of information in the compiling of this work. The labours of its past editors, Don Rojas and Brian Meeks, plus journalists Earl Bousquet, Keith Jeremiah, Garvin Stuart, Patsy Lewis, Camille Ramnarace and Vivian Philbert have made a valuable contribution to what follows in these pages. I also thank Arthur Winner, Wayne Carter and Kevin Williams, photographers of the Revolution, whose work has provided the visual dimension of this book, and the poets and calypsonians whom I have quoted.

INTRODUCTION

On March 25th 1983, President Ronald Reagan announced, in the words of an editorial in *The Times* of London, 'one of the most fundamental switches in American strategic concepts since the Second World War'. It was a plan to build a space laser 'umbrella' around the United States as a 'defensive' measure against hostile missiles. This new dimension of 'Star Wars' military technology was necessary, said Reagan, because of an increased threat to U.S. national security coming directly from the Caribbean Basin. Suddenly, as if as evidence for this, there was projected behind Reagan an aerial photograph of the site of Point Salines International Airport, Grenada, with the President suggesting that no country of Grenada's size 'which hasn't even got an air force' would build such an airport unless it was for sinister military purposes.

As the President spoke, U.S. trained and financed counter-revolutionary forces were penetrating Nicaragua in a new assault on the revolution and massive American military assistance was continuing to flow to the repressive El Salvador government facing the armed resistance of the people. Simultaneously, military manoeuvres organised by NATO were taking place in the Eastern Caribbean, including 77 American, British and Dutch warships and 300 aircraft, with the intention, in the words of the U.S. Navy Secretary Lehman, 'of reflecting the lessons learned from the Falklands war'. Grenada in particular was constantly harassed and threatened, with U.S. warships approaching to within ten kilometres of the airport site at Point Salines.

Thus the world was learning about Grenada, and was soon learning more, as Reagan's assertions and the warmongering of his navy were being continually rebuffed and exposed, even in his domestic American press, by democratically-motivated journalists who were intent upon telling the truth: that the World Bank itself had declared that Grenada's economy could not hope to grow without a new civil airport; that the runway's length was, in fact, nine thousand feet and not ten thousand feet as Reagan had told the world; that various other islands in the Caribbean including St. Lucia, Trinidad, Martinique, Guadeloupe, Barbados and Curaçao had longer runways and Antigua and Aruba runways of an equal length; that the airport was being built with the help of sixteen nations including a dredging firm from Miami, U.S.A. whose workers worked side-by-side with Grenadians and Cuban internationalists; that at the end of the runway stood a private U.S. medical school whose students regularly used it as a jogging track; that despite the President's aerial photographs taken by spy planes illegally flying over Grenada's air space, any tourist, American or otherwise, could take as many holiday snapshots as they wished, alongside the hundreds of Grenadians having weekend picnics and flying their kites over the runway.

The Grenada Revolution, begun on March 13th, 1979, has had to struggle against every such conceivable method of destabilization harnessed against it by the U.S. Government. Here is a tiny Caribbean country, twenty miles long and ten miles wide, with two tinier sister islands, the home of some 110,000 people, being systematically and continually bullied by the world's greatest economic and military power. Grenada's crime? A creative, independent spirit and a government that loves and respects its people and breathes every second a will to free them from underdevelopment and four hundred years of economic dependence and institutional mimicry.

Of course, the first reaction to any revolutionary process by the enemies of the revolution has always been destabilization and intervention. Every popular revolutionary government has had to consolidate itself and build its process and simultaneously deal with relentless attacks and attempts to turn it back. Thus, in the case of Grenada and its people, 'destabilization' is not just a word and a new addition to the Caribbean vocabulary. It means definite things. It means murder, arson, bombs, lies, slander, threats, intimidation, mercenary menace and attempts to snatch away all the concrete and popular benefits won through the revolution over the last five years:

from free milk to house repair, from university scholarships to agro-industries, from free health care to an end to illiteracy, from a huge decline in unemployment to a 5.5% growth rate in the national economy.

This book starts out with two main objectives. The first is to seek to itemise, categorise and describe the various approaches and strategies of destabilization used primarily by U.S. government agencies against Grenada. Such a task has, of course, been done before in relation to other nations that have faced the same enemy, and with particular regard to the Caribbean the reader is urged to consult Cheddi Jagan's *The West on Trial* and Michael Manley's *Jamaica: The Struggle in the Periphery*, for a thorough grounding in two previous courageous stands against the might of U.S. destabilization.

The other objective, however, is even more crucial. How is Grenada so successfully standing up against this bombardment being hurled against it? How are its people educating themselves, organising themselves and mobilising themselves to beat back their enemies and to continue to build their revolution? What part do the organs of the new democracy play in this process? How does the explosion of revolutionary culture provide a new energy to withstand these provocations? How are the people educating themselves about the true cause and nature of destabilization? What is the role of the Militia? These questions, I hope, will be partially answered within these pages, for as Grenada is constantly learning from what is happening in the rest of the world, her experiences of the last five years have also much to teach it.

When Michael Manley's *Jamaica: The Struggle in the Periphery*, which is companion to this present volume, was launched in Grenada, the author had these words to say to the Grenadian people about their revolution:

> Where an internal process is united and has adequate mass foundation, you could bring all the C.I.A.'s in the world and they would not advance one inch because they would be rebuffed by the unity of the people themselves. And that is why, with all the pressures to which you are subject, I dare to predict with confidence that no such force will prevail against the Grenada Revolution.
>
> One of the reasons why I have the deepest commitment and gratitude is in observing your own unswerving concentration upon general education and, above all, upon political education. I think

that is one of the critical strengths of the Grenadian process . . . I think that you are engaged in something that is critical, something that is commanding the attention of progressive people everywhere in the world. And I say to all of you, guard what you are doing jealously! You have already made a notable contribution. You have made the name of Grenada carry a significance that is astonishing having regard to your actual size, proving that importance in the world is not guaranteed by size, but by consistency, originality and dedication to those objectives that are relevant. You are a light of significant hope in the Caribbean to many, many tens of thousands of people. Keep that light burning!

PART 1: FROM CROWN COLONY TO PEOPLE'S REVOLUTION

This Revolution is for work, for food, for decent housing and health services, and for a bright future for our children and grandchildren.
Maurice Bishop: Address to the Grenadian People, 13 March
1979

SUCH CONCRETE and real social benefits have always been the basic aspirations of the Caribbean people, have always been their consistent objectives of struggle. The people of Grenada, the southernmost of the Windward Islands, had through four centuries of colonial rule been a vital and integral part of that energy of resistance. During these years they had struck blow after blow for their freedom and had produced both movements and individuals of genuine originality and genius. In 1650, Grenada's Caribs jumped into the sea over a high cliff, having fought right across the mountainous spine of their island, rather than surrender to the French colonialists, and their example was emulated many times in the revolts of the plantation slaves. These struggles reached their climax in the 1795 revolt led by Julien Fedon, a free planter, who, inspired by the French and Haitian Revolutions, and working in close liaison with the Caribbean apostle of Revolution, Victor Hughes, controlled the island for two years, only being defeated after British colonialism had called upon its Spanish allies in Trinidad to lend reinforcements. The emancipation of the Grenadian slaves did not tame the drive towards freedom and true political justice, and in 1848 the Parish of St Patrick's was ablaze with organized indignation and rebellion as the plantocracy moved to reduce the wages of agricultural labourers.

Before the halfway point of the present century, out of

Grenada had come two outstanding Caribbean figures. The first was the pioneer West Indian federalist, T Albert Marryshow. For fifty years he campaigned for the realization of his dream of Caribbean unity, as journalist, trade unionist and politician. He broke through the colonial armour in 1921 after a lone journey to London to secure a measure of representation in the Legislative Councils which exerted the local power in the British Crown Colony system, and this was won not only for Grenada, but also in Trinidad and the other Windward and Leeward Islands, finally resulting in the establishment of the short-lived Federation of the West Indies in 1958, also the year of Marryshow's death. Whist the 'Father of Federation' was labouring to unite the Caribbean in one political structure, another Grenadian, Tubal Uriah 'Buzz' Butler, brought together and unionized the Trinidadian oilworkers, laying the foundation for an enduring mass workers' movement in the explosive strikes of 1937 and giving further impetus to the anti-colonial struggle throughout the Caribbean which, over the next two decades, was to be led to political independence in Trinidad by Dr Eric Williams and the People's National Movement.

1951 and its Aftermath

By 1950 Grenada had reached a certain conjunction of contradictions, which, when rubbed together would spark off great upsurge and change. The Plantocracy, composed largely of the descendants of the slaveowners, still controlled two-thirds of the richest cultivated land in the island. This ownership was complemented by their participation in the colonial state machinery. They were allowed two of the members on the three-member Legislative Council which operated directly below the government-appointed Executive Council. Their estates comprised at least fifty acres, and this contrasted starkly with the small-holdings of up to five acres of the ten thousand peasant farmers. Their land, generally given over to the three cash crops of bananas, nutmegs and cocoa, was also of a much poorer quality. A very small national capitalist class owned the few factories and import and retail agencies in St George's, the main urban centre. Thus the balance of the population was engaged primarily in agricultural labour on the large private estates, working in woeful conditions that had not changed substantially since the time of emancipation, and earning a mere eighty-two cents a day. These paltry wages were linked peril-ously to the world market prices of the export crops, an arrangement entered into by the Grenada Trade Union Coun-cil, which kept docilely in line with the Employers' Society.

Towards the end of 1950, the world prices of cocoa fell and the wages of the agricultural workers plummeted accordingly. The requests of the TUC to the employers to forego a wages reduction met with a stony refusal. This was accompanied by a campaign by certain estate owners to evict workers who had been squatting on land belonging to the estates. Thus the issues of wages and land, fused by the arrogant racism of the over-whelmingly white and mulatto plantocracy towards the black work force, created the scenario for a release of pent-up anger and determination which erupted in February 1951, as 'Sky Red' flamed through the island.

Into this situation had walked Eric Matthew Gairy, an ex-schoolteacher and ne'er-do-well from a village in St Andrew's. He had, like many Grenadians of his generation, emigrated to the Dutch-owned island of Aruba in the late 1940s to work in the American oil refineries, but his flamboyant involvement in organizing workers there had resulted in his deportation to Grenada in 1950. He carried the flint of trade union experience into the parched forest of downtrodden agricultural workers. By July 1950 he had formed his Grenada Manual and Mental Workers' Union and also a political party, the Grenada People's Party, which later became the Grenada United Labour Party. His highly individualistic and charismatic approach to trade union organization, which later was to prove so gangrenous, had an immediate success with the long-oppressed agro-proletariat who were avidly looking for leadership. Conse-quently, Gairy was able not only to lead and direct the course of the workers' anger, but channel it exactly where he wanted it to go, towards his own self-aggrandizement. Mass popular will and urge for change was squeezed into his mould. On 21 February 1957, after leading a demonstration to the offices of the Legislative Council in St George's, Gairy was arrested with his lieutenant, Gascoyne Blaize, detained first on a British warship and then on the sister island of Carriacou. But by 5 March he had been released, his trade union had been recog-nized and he was negotiating with the colonial governor to bring the popular revolt to heel. By this time the masses had turned towards government targets with their organized arson, which had included Belmont Government School and the Governor's own bathing hut!

Treating his supporters like mischievous children, Gairy berated them publicly at a mass meeting organized with full co-operation of the Governor:

> I have promised His Excellency the Governor, there shall be no more acts of violence in Grenada . . . Do you trust me? Well say after me now: 'I swear before God and man that I shall not commit any acts of violence and if I know . . .' Just a minute! If there is someone near to you who does not put his hand up, let his name go to the police. '. . . I shall not commit any act of violence, and if I know of anyone who commits any act of violence or acts of violence, I shall report to the Union head, before God and man – so help me God!'[1]

Such talk was reinforced a week later when the colonial propaganda apparatus was given over to 'Uncle Gairy' to reiterate his appeasement in an islandwide broadcast: ('Join me in saying "No more violence!" Come on now, those of you listening, let's say "No more violence!" three times together: "No more violence, no more violence, no more violence!" Thank you.'). The words smothered a rebellion that had proved to be irrepressible by not only the local police force and that of St Lucia too, but also by the Royal Marines. By October of the same year the first universal adult franchise elections had been held and Gairy himself was Chief Minister, sitting in the seat of power he had carved out for himself. It had been a skilful opportunistic performance, carried out on the backs of the agro-proletariat, who after some temporary advances and increase in wages, soon found themselves once again in their previous conditions. As one woman agricultural worker reflected thirty years later:

> We fought a revolution in 1951 and then Gairy sell we over. He sell we over to the big bourgeois, even though we struggle hard. I remember when shell was blowing and men with cocoa knife and women with cutlass and basket all going to the estate in Marlmount to pick cocoa for weself. We didn't frighten even though the estate owner call a bus of police, and they shoot at we and later they kill three of we. But Gairy forget we and things get worse. His never union help we, they just taking all we money and we not getting anything back.[2]

The mass action of the agricultural workers in 1951 meant that they now had a basis for organization, despite Gairy's habitual sell-outs of his main supporters to those estate owners who were prepared to co-operate with him. The plantocracy as a class never recovered their previous overweening self-confidence and arrogance. In 1955 the ravages of Hurricane Janet speeded up their gradual decay as an economic force and this disintegration was accompanied by Gairy's conscious building of a new commercial class, whose burgeoning interests his Grenada United Labour Party came to represent. Gairy himself, as he began to acquire enterprise after enterprise and hotel after hotel through widespread corruption, led the way as the new class's main protagonist. The cause of the agricultural workers was discarded as Gairy made his new alliance with medium and large businessmen and various transnational Caribbean firms like Kirpalani's, Geddes Grant and Y de Lima. The rural masses were left shattered and bewildered, as Renalph Gebon describes in his 'Ballad of the Estate Worker':

> Strike dun
> We had we fun,
> De price rise,
> Well, now we ha' to cry:
> Ah ten cent yah
> Ah ten cent day,
> All from we pay.
> Freeness dun . . .
> While the big boss,
> E feeding fat:
> War ah do dat far?
> For me to suffer?
> And one man flourish
> While we dee followers perish?[3]

Thus the national bourgeoisie, as small as it was became split. The more aggressive 'newer' sections forged ahead with Gairy, gaining various concessions, favours and government contracts, while the older merchant class made a strategic alliance with the decaying plantocrats, playing out their swansong with the formation of the Grenada National Party in 1955. Despite the historical decrepitude of this party, led by Herbert A Blaize, Gairy's peculations and abuses of power became so rife and public that he fell from office in the 1957 elections and the

GNP formed a coalition government from 1957 to 1961. Then, after Gairy had been returned in 1961, his 'Squandermania' became so scandalous that fifteen months later the GNP were back by default and were to stay in power until 1967, when Gairy was to return, rampant again.

Gairyism

The 'Squandermania' scandal became black and white fact in 1962 with the publication of the Report of the Commission of Enquiry into the Control of Public Expenditure. It revealed intimidation of public workers, the licensing of corruption and a massive redirection of public funds into the personal coffers of Gairy and his aspirant businessmen supporters. Such abuses became the permanent backcloth to Gairyism. It was characterized by an intensely *personal* control and execution of power, which meant, whether in a government or trade union context, that Gairy would constantly promote himself as a messianic, indispensable force. Towards the end of his career, he was to express this publicly with his customary verbosity and sense of divine rectitude:

> Ladies and gentlemen, considering the size of Grenada and the odds against which we have always been constrained to work, I am sure — and I know you will agreed with me — that the national growth and development of our new and vibrant nation, the meaningful contribution and the impactful and efficacious thrust we make in matters of Regional and International proportions could not have been possible without God's Inspiration, His Protection and Guidance. Certainly, some of the contributions we have been making in the context of man's relation to man, man's relation to his natural habitat — his Planet Earth — and the awakening of man's consciousness, have transcended beyond the externals of man, and indeed, today we are asking the peoples of our world to reach out with us even beyond the boundaries of our global limitations . . .
>
> It was through God's Inspiration that in 1970 Grenada participated in the 'Miss World' Beauty Contest, through which our own charming Jennifer Hosten, who emerged as 'Miss World 1970–71', successfully portraying the undeniable charm, the inward glow and magnetism characterising the inimitable warmth of the people of Grenada, and drew thousands of visitors to our shores in their

search for this 'Small Island' paradise whence came such talent, such charm and such beauty. Indeed, Grenada's ambassadors on that memorable occasion in November 1970, included not only Jennifer, but also her equally charming sister Pamela, now Mrs Bruce Procope, who acted as chaperone, and Mrs Gert Protain of the Grenada Tourist Board, whose description of the touristic potential of our dear land succeeded in attracting many people to our shores . . .

It was through Divine Inspiration, that we raised in the United Nations the concept of the Universality of God, and called upon other Leaders of the world — Political, Spiritual, Mystical, Philosophical, Religious among others — to accept the concept and apply it on a regular day-to-day basis. It was that same Divine Inspiration that led me to introduce in Grenada, a National Day of Prayer and Thanksgiving on which all Grenada citizens, residents and visiting friends are called to go to our Creator in humility and thank Him for all His Blessings unceasingly being showered upon us. Indeed, the motto of Grenada reflects this recognition and acceptance of God, and I quote: 'Ever conscious of God, We Aspire, Build and Advance as One People'. It was through Divine Inspiration that I was motivated to install, on the most prominent site overlooking our capital city, a large Holy Cross as a Symbol of Christianity and a beacon to those at sea. It dawned on me a few days ago that the white bulbs on the Cross should be changed to purple to reflect the Passion and Agony of Christ. But I was advised (by Mr Glyn Evans) against this course of action since seamen have now become accustomed to our beautifully lighted Cross as their established beacon which can be identified some fifty miles at sea, and any change of its brilliance or colour would definitely present some confusion.

It was through Divine Inspiration that Grenada raised at the United Nations the question of the occurrence of strange and seemingly inexplicable psychic and related phenomena which continue to baffle man, and I cited the Bermuda Triangle as but one example. Many persons who heard my address might have considered my presentation as being somewhat extraneous, but it was interesting to note that it was only last year that the two major powers of the world — the United States and Russia — initiated a joint project to look into that very phenomenon of the Bermuda Triangle — a most turbulent water-grave that has snatched the life of so many human beings, and so many aircraft and ships.

It was that same Divine Inspiration which in 1976 led me to raise at the United Nations the subject of UFOs and related phenomena and called upon that world body to establish an agency or depart-ment to take some action and co-ordinate international research . . . This is undoubtedly a great achievement for our small country which has only been possible because of Divine Guidance.[4]

Gairy's obscurantism, like that of his ally Duvalier of Haiti, promoted *obeah* and superstition among the rural masses. While he betrayed the agricultural workers and peculated their union dues, rifled the National Treasury, helped to build up the local arm of imperialism by his promotion of multinational interests, took his customary percentage from every govern-ment deal he was engaged in, allowed roads, schools and hospitals to crumble and collapse around him, stole the animals of poor people to be consumed on his 'Meet the People' tours or parties at his 'Evening Palace' and other gaudy brothels, arranged for beatings and 'disappearances' of his opponents and critics and the sexual victimization and mistreatment of two generations of Grenadian women — he wrote prayers to be printed in their thousands at the Government Printery:

Holy Father, God of the cosmic, universal God, you know better than we do, the task is not yet over and so we ask you to calm our enemies as Christ calmed the tempest in the Sea of Galilee. We ask you Dear Father to forgive them all for their efforts in trying to bring down the Government or in trying to embarrass the Gov-ernment or in trying to obstruct the attainment of full independence for our country and its people. We ask forgiveness for them through Jesus Christ our Redeemer. Guide, protect and defend us from this time forward from all our enemies both visible and invisible as you have always guided us: protect and defend us should our enemies continue in any efforts designed to obstruct our progress and the prosperity of this State, we pray dear Father to remove them from our path and deal with them accordingly; deal with them as Thou seest fit.

Have mercy upon our Prime Minister Designate, Eric Matthew Gairy, remove from him all dark, evil and negative conditions that may be around him; any evil force that may try to tie him down or weigh him down or burden him in any way or tend to prevent him to perform his obligations more promptly and more effectively. Save him from all danger and all malice, jealousy and hate of his enemies. Save him from their arms, weapons and whatever plots and schemes they may formulate against him . . .

This was no mindless babbling. For Gairy was consciously creating a smokescreen of superstition and irrationality to cover his own corrupt tracks laying as he did so the emotive base for violent anti-communism:

> This period of our history requires that every single one of us, young as well as old, to be loyal and patriotic to our new nation for we have to guard against the evils of communism. We have to guard against Grenada becoming a seat of atheistic ideologies and philosophies.[5]

The same religiosity was allied to his political tribalism, and he became more terrifyingly adept at dividing his people than even his tutors, the British colonialists, had been. A typical example of this was organized in Carriacou in 1972. This parish had never supported Gairy's party, and had been a base of the GNP as the home of Blaize. In 1972 the sister island experienced a ferocious drought, which Gairy exploited with all his obscurantist tricks to exacerbate division amongst the people. He declared a 'Day of Prayer' for an end to the drought, which his Secretary for Carriacou and Petit Martinique Affairs, Michael Caesar, proclaimed through a broadsheet, featuring a grotesque pun on the name of the leader of the opposition party.

A DAY OF PRAYER

My dear people of Carriacou and Petit Martinique, this is a time for prayers and repentance. Today, we are experiencing one of the longest and most devastating droughts of our history — a drought which, like a blaize of fire has destroyed all our crops.

To those of us who believe in God, in the Truth, the Light and the Way, this is a calamity which represents some form of punishment. Some people are asking what have we done to deserve such punishment? I am sure that you will agree with me that God in His Righteousness would never suffer a people who is living according to His way.

Yes my dear people, the time has come for us to examine our conscience and try to determine what we have done, or what wrong we have committed to deserve such terrible punishment.

Referring to this Blaize-of-fire drought which has completely destroyed all our crops, and of the wrongs which we have committed, I am reminded of an incident which took place here in Carriacou immediately following the last elections, I refer to a tractor, which, I understand was brought to Carriacou specifically to plough the lands of only those who voted or supported the Grenada National Party. I understand further that several Carriacouans who were suspected of having voted for or supported the Grenada United Labour Party or the Government were bluntly refused the rented service of that tractor. Consequently, only lands belonging to GNP supporters in Carriacou were ploughed and prepared for the expected annual rainy season . . .

Take warning, my dear people, and remember that we, as human beings, can fool one another, but we cannot fool God. In Carriacou today, there are a number of organizations that are being operated under the guise of social, cultural or even charitable intentions, but you know as well as I do, that their motives are very sinister and contrary to what the organizers profess them to be. You know too, that certain persons have been going around by night and day, telling lies, preaching hate, and like wolves in sheep clothing have been deceiving the poor people and robbing them of their much needed pennies, under false pretences. Beware, my dear people, and again remember that they are only fooling themselves, because we believe that there is a just God Whom they cannot fool.

Obviously, this terrible drought situation is a consequence of the sinful way of life which prevails in Carriacou and Petit Martinique today. This sinful way of hate, of violence, of ungratefulness and of untruth, is NOT the Way of God, but of men who represent the devil and his followers, and consequently are responsible for summoning the wrath of God upon us all.[6]

The Growth of a new Opposition: the 'Jewel'

The 1970 Black Power upsurge in Trinidad found a huge empathy in Grenada. Many of the 55 per cent of the population who were unemployed were casualties of the decay and disintegration of the large estates and were eager to listen to the voices of rebellion they heard coming so stridently from Trinidad, where many of their relatives had gone years before in search of work. Simultaneously, a generation of Grenadians who had been educated in universities abroad, and who had experienced and struggled against racism in Europe and North America, was returning home. They had been a part of solidarity movements for the national liberation struggles in Vietnam and Southern Africa. They had developed first-hand experience in organizing. They had arrived at a firm world view and an unequivocal anti-imperialist consciousness. They rejected parochial and tribal politics and had lived and studied among oppressed peoples from all over the world. Their activities abroad formed an apprenticeship to what they realized would be a life-or-death struggle on their return home.

Maurice Bishop, for example, helped to found the first Legal Aid Centre for Caribbean people in Notting Hill, West London, and Bernard Coard campaigned tirelessly against racism in education in the same city, writing a book called *How the West Indian Child is Made Educationally Sub-normal in the British School System*, which had a seminal effect among black parents and London teachers. Such men had a vision of a new kind of society to the one they had grown up in: they had read of and studied the Cuban Revolution, Nyerere's approaches in Tanzania, the struggles of the African Liberation Movements, the strategic genius of the Vietnamese war of liberation. They had sat in the front row to study every word and gesture of Malcolm X — himself of Grenadian parentage — when he visited London in 1964 and, most importantly, they had studied their own Grenadian history and the heroic contributions of Fedon and Marryshow. Although they had come from petit-bourgeois origins, their identification was totally with the oppressed, the betrayed agricultural masses and peasants, the unemployed urban and rural youth and the small but growing working class in their country. These men, like Maurice Bishop, Kenrick Radix, Unison Whiteman and Bernard Coard, were to create a new vision for the Caribbean; and when that vision was married to the concrete struggle of the workers and peasants and the relentless energy of the working class activists like Selwyn Strachan, George Louison, Hudson Austin and Vincent Noel who were to dynamize that struggle, the vision would come to reality.

To Gairy they were anathema, the 'Johnny-come-lately Jewellers'. He could only splutter with rage when he spoke of them: 'These irresponsible malcontents, these disgruntled political frustrates coming from abroad, whether it be university or otherwise — coming here, metaphorically and literally hot and sweaty, and shouting "Power to the People" . . .'[7]

These new elements took a full and organizational part in the Black Power solidarity demonstration which shook St George's in May 1970. Gairy's frightened response was to pass an

Emergency Powers Act, giving him the right to search without warrant, limit public assemblies and confiscate literature. He also declared that he would double the existing police force, boasting that he had established a special squad of the 'roughest and toughest roughnecks' to give him personal protection and who were to become solely accountable to him. This group soon became infamous as the Mongoose Gang and was quickly despatched against demonstrating nurses in December, 1970.

The nurses had finally become militant with disgust at hospitals which had no sheets, no aspirin, infestations of rats and reputations as charnel houses. As their demonstration was violently broken up, Bishop and Whiteman, who had given them their active support, were arrested alongside them. When the nurses were summarily dismissed and permanently victimized, Gairy's comments in a radio broadcast were: 'Why should taxpayers' money go to idle young women who choose to jump in the streets like *jour ouvert* masqueraders? . . . If they like to demonstrate like masqueraders and to protest at every single thing, we like it better. If they like to spend a month or so in court, we love it too. My police officers can spare time in court watching them and guiding them to the public facilities when they require to use them.'[8]

Maurice Bishop had been one of the founders of FORUM, a group of radical professionals which grew out of the Black Power solidarity movement and which sought to lay the basis for a new political party in Grenada. It was, however, short-lived and succeeded in early 1972 by the Movement for the Advancement of Community Effort, (MACE), which set as its immediate objectives political research and education. But it was the subsequent organization, the Movement of Assemblies for the People (MAP), which developed in the latter part of the same year, which laid the basis for real political organization and activity — and already had its prime objective the gaining of state power and an alternative model of democracy to the Westminster colonial apparatus. While MAP was seeking to involve the urban youth, the Joint Endeavour for the Welfare, Education and Liberation of the People (JEWEL), led by Unison Whiteman, was organizing in the rural parish of St David's, the traditional stronghold of Gairy's erstwhile supporters, the agricultural labourers.

It was also in St David's Parish that the two organizations were effectively synthesized through struggle. In late 1972,

with the apparent approval of Gairy, an English peer, Lord
Brownlow, cut off popular access to the beach of La Sagesse
which bordered his estate. Gairy ignored the loud protests
coming from the people, who turned directly to the young
militants of MAP and JEWEL. These organized and led the
1,000-strong demonstration. Lord Brownlow's offensive barrier was torn down and a People's Trial condemned the peer as
unwanted in Grenada. In March 1973, the two organizations
formally merged to form the New Jewel Movement.

The new party was soon to be blooded. In April 1973, an
unemployed young man of St Andrew's from a family of
Gairy's supporters — Jeremiah Richardson — was killed in cold
blood by a bullet to the temple by one of Gairy's police outside
the De Luxe Cinema in Grenville. It was a totally wanton act of
butchery that raised enormous indignation and protest in the
east coast town, which numbered amongst its population many
of Gairy's former supporters. Five thousand people marched to
Grenville Police Station and, having seen the police flee in all
directions, continued to Pearls' Airport, where they closed
down flights for three days. Gairy was livid and tried to soothe
the situation by a national broadcast:

> In the first case, the dead young man, his parents and relatives are all
> members of, and friends of our Trade Union, and to our Political
> Party. We have given them some help, and in the final analysis, it is
> the same Labour Government and the same Grenada Manual and
> Mental Workers' Union, or I personally, who will have to come to
> their rescue to provide them with help that is both substantial and
> meaningful.[9]

It clearly would not work. He then, desperately, sought to
invoke the 'prophets' and his own political career to try to gain
favour:

> I will NOT, I repeat NOT, be ruffled, or excited by any threats, any
> demands, or any demonstration whatsoever in the exercise of my
> responsibility to the State. I was born to do the job that I am doing
> today. I am the 'Little Man from the East' who spoke from the almond
> tree on the seaside at Grenville in 1950 when I came on the
> Grenada political scene. I am the man referred to by the prophet
> McLawrence, and also Mrs de Coteau. I have passed through the
> oven — battleships were brought here with the hope that my
> assignment may be thwarted. About fifty-two police cases were

given me in one year . . . but I didn't cower, I didn't crouch, I didn't bow. I was threatened to be shot by scores of employers. I happened to be the only man in the entire West Indies whose *bona fide* franchise was taken away.[10]

It was a solo performance of pathetic panic, of a dictator losing his grip, and it signalled a definite watershed in the struggle of the Grenadian people. The New Jewel Movement began to prosper and their confidence was lifted with the slogan that appeared on the front page of their manifesto issued in November of 1973: 'We'll be free in '73'.

The Manifesto set out the projected parameters of a 'new society'. It spoke of primary health care; of low-cost housing schemes; of a national food strategy; of free secondary education and a new curriculum; of an agricultural revolution and the development of agro-industries; of a regeneration of Carriacou and Petit Martinique — 'the forgotten islands'; of nationalization; of full employment; national insurance; 'people's courts'; a non-aligned foreign policy and support for the national liberation movements; real independence rather than the change-of-flag routine that Gairy was presently engaged in; and geniune people's democracy and assemblies to replace the Westminster charade: 'No government can continue to function in the face of the organized opposition and mobilization of the people,' the Manifesto argued on its final page: 'When a government ceases to serve the people and instead steals from and exploits the people at every turn, the people are entitled to dissolve it and replace it by any means necessary.'[11] Gairy and imperialism were warned: 13 March 1979 was already on the Caribbean agenda.

The 'Crisis': November 1973–April 1974

Gairy, the King of the island
Ordered everyone to adhere to his command.
'Bring the champagne, wine and whisky to Evening Palace!
Don't forget the truck load of yams!
Make haste — full pace!
Beat up the opposition band while I'm gone!'
Enter the town with buttoo and 303 guns!
Break, enter and take down to burn, burn!

Elections? That's ours all the time!

Brutality was raging with a mist of copper-bruised sky —
It made me shiver
To see bloodstained streets,
And angry babylons galloped with batons and 303 guns
When injustice was proclaimed.[12]

The next few months were to create a whirlwind of action and reaction. While in London Gairy, accompanied by Blaize, discussed paper independence—which was formally attained in February, 1974 — in Grenada the anti-Gairy arm of the bourgeoisie, led by the local Chamber of Commerce, fomented a brief general strike and a series of demonstrations. This was supported by thousands of school-children and the fast-growing town unions centred in St George's, like the Commercial and Industrial Workers' Union, the Technical and Allied Workers' Union — both of which had started as a result of frustration and protest at the despotic and corrupt farce of the Grenada Manual and Mental Workers' Union — and the Seamen and Waterfront Workers' Union. The leadership of these new unions was anti-Gairy, but was equally terrified of the prospect of real workers' power and democracy. They thus went no further than the feeble alternative offered by the Grenada National Party. Then, on 4 November, following up their People's Convention on the independence issue in May, which had attracted some fifteen thousand people, the New Jewel Movement organized a similarly massive People's Congress in Seamoon Stadium, near Grenville. Gairyism was pilloried as the dictator, charged with twenty-seven crimes against the Grenadian people, was called upon to resign. The Hon Prime Minister, extremely upset that his personal kudos for bringing what the NJM called 'meaningless' independence to Grenada was being undermined, could only answer: 'This is trash! The damage these wicked people have done at home and abroad to our country and our people is irrepairable, and perhaps unpardonable.'

The actions that accompanied these words signalled the intensified fascist direction of Gairy's rule over the country. The NJM had declared that a general strike would be called if Gairy failed to resign. Then on 18 November, when the strike was due to begin, Grenadians experienced what later came to be known as 'Bloody Sunday':

Bloody Sunday we shall never forget,
When them rabid mongoose get out their net . . .[13]

One of the victims of that day, Selwyn Strachan, now Minister of National Mobilization, tells the story of its grim events:

On that Sunday morning, Comrade Hudson Austin came by my home and told me that Grenville businessman H M Bhola, would like the NJM to meet with the businessmen in Grenville to explain in a detailed way the nature of the general shut-down which was supposed to take place the following day, the Monday, 19 November 1973. It was on that basis that we agreed that all of us — Comrades Bishop, Radix, Whiteman, Austin, Daniel and myself — should go up in the afternoon. The meeting was organised by Bhola and was due to take place at the De Luxe Cinema in Grenville.

At around one o'clock that Sunday, we all gathered at Comrade Bishop's home to hold a final discussion on the content of the meeting so that there would be no doubt after we finished the meeting on how things would go the following day. We used three cars to go to Grenville. Whilst we were preparing to leave from Comrade Bishop's home, there were quite a few secret police and regular police outside waiting to follow us. We had to dodge and escape from them, and were able to lose sight of them after a while. We got into Grenville between 2.30 and 3.00 pm, and when we arrived at the scene where the meeting was supposed to be held, the De Luxe Cinema, we were confronted by plain-clothes policemen and secret police fully armed with pickaxe handles.

We could not have entered the yard because it was taken over by dozens of secret police and plain-clothes policemen who were more or less leading the operation. Bhola, who was on the scene, suggested to us that we should transfer the meeting to his home. We agreed to that because we were prepared to avoid the confrontation. Whilst we were at his home waiting for the other businessmen to arrive, and discussing what we have just encountered at the cinema, Comrade Daniel walked across to one of the shops, but had to rush back after the secret police he had met there started to threaten him.

Suddenly, more and more secret police began to gather up and encircle the place. After that had reached a certain level, Inspector Innocent Belmar suddenly arrived on the scene, got out of the car and ordered his secret police to get us. His exact words were: 'Get them dogs!' He also fired off a couple of bullets. Comrades Radix, Austin and Daniel were able to make a quick dash upstairs and escape the secret police. Comrades Bishop, Whiteman and I were further away from the steps and were unable to make a quick escape from the secret police using the same route, but had to go around the building trying to escape from them. Whilst the three of us were hiding from them behind a piece of wall, they started to fire at us, with bullets flying on the sides and over our heads. We think it was because they were not properly trained that they did not penetrate us with bullets. As soon as we got out from behind the wall, they converged on us immediately, beating us from there into the streets, and separated us from each other. We did not see each other again until hours later in the cell in the Grenville Police Station.

We were beaten unconscious, fell, regained consciousness, fell again and were then dragged through the streets by the secret police into the police station. There the plain-clothes and secret policemen were ordered to shave us and collect the blood that was flowing from our bodies. They actually threatened us to drink the blood which they collected. All three of us were there, bleeding in the cell because they had shaved us with broken bottles and the blood continued to flow from our bodies. The other three comrades were also shaved and thrown in the cell with us.

Throughout the night we were tortured by Belmar and the secret police who had taken over from the plain-clothes policemen. From time to time, Belmar would come and order us to get up and sit down, under much pain. I could recall that Comrade Austin had Comrade Bishop in his lap, bleeding profusely. The underpants Comrade Austin was wearing changed colour from white to red. It was a night of terror.

Next morning, we were handcuffed and taken to a Grenville magistrate's court where we were charged with attempting to overthrow the régime. Magistrate I Duncan, on the orders of Gairy, sent us to jail.

At the prison, for the first time since our beating, we saw a doctor. So we are talking about more than a day later. He sent us immediately to hospital.

The people were outraged by this barbarous act of the Gairy dictatorship and were annoyed that such treatment was meted out to the party's leadership. That incident sparked off the mass democratic protest that took place in the ensuing months, when people from all walks of life were calling upon Gairy to resign. From that brutal incident, the people never turned back.[14]

Bloody Sunday had a profound effect on all strata opposed to Gairy in Grenada. Twenty-two organizations proclaiming themselves to be 'non-political' came together to organize an island-wide shutdown which signalled the 'crisis'. The so-called 'Committee of 22' included the Churches, the Employers' Federation and the Chamber of Commerce. Their main demand was not the removal of Gairy, but a curbing of what they saw were his excesses, in particular the 'police aides'. There were some sections, however, who were toying with the strategy of replacing the embarrassing and volatile Gairy with the more predictable and pliable George Hosten, Gairy's Minister of Finance. They were certainly not seeking any change in the current class interest, but merely a less vulgar front man. But Gairy's private protectors made sure of his continued entrenchment. NJM activists were being hounded and attacked while their leaders lay battered in hospital and, on 27 December, Harold Strachan, a taxi driver and party militant who was acting as security to Bishop, Whiteman and Strachan, was gunned to death by the Mongoose Gang.

The repression continued unabated into the new year, when on 1 January the dockworkers began their three-month strike. As dockworkers and schoolchildren marched around St George's every day, they gained more and more sympathy and support. The climax came on 21 January when the Mongoose Gang and the Green Beast troops, together with other Gairy hoodlums, stormed into Otway House, the headquarters of the Seamen and Waterfront Workers' Union on the Carenage, or Inner Harbour, attacking demonstrators and finally killing Rupert Bishop, small businessman and father of Maurice, as he barred the doorway and protected a room full of women and schoolchildren. His widow, Mrs. Alimenta Bishop, remembers:

> Every day, every day he would be demonstrating, walking along the road on the outside of the schoolchildren. Then on the twenty-first, someone told him not to go, that there would be real trouble that day. But Rupert responded: 'No, don't tell people that! If you tell them that they won't go to the demonstration. It is better to die on your feet than to creep on your knees all the days of your life.'

When the first schoolchild was hurt on the demonstration, when Gairy's men came along the Carenage with bottles, stones and guns, Rupert threw the keys of his car to Kenrick Radix and told him to drive the child directly to the hospital for attention.

Upstairs in Otway House the people were taking refuge, particularly women and schoolchildren. Rupert sat behind the door, jamming it shut and preventing it from being opened. Then they broke the door and, as he stood up to block the doorway, they shot him point blank, as the tear gas smothered the room and the people inside were coughing and choking.[15]

As the strike continued, more and more sections became involved. Fuel in the state became exhausted, no tax revenue was being collected and civil servants and sections of the police were beginning to show progressive sympathies with the strikers. The GNP-inclined trade union leadership, particularly within the SWWU was clearly becoming alarmed at the militancy and self-organization of their own rank and file. When $45,000 strike sustenance arrived from Grenadians abroad, threatening to take the strike to a successful conclusion, then enough was enough! This backward leadership, an element of which had been trained by the predecessor of the American Institute for Free Labor Development, the labour arm of the U.S. State Department directly connected to the C.I.A., capitulated on the brink of victory, supported by the leadership of the Caribbean Congress of Labour. With the spearhead of the strike now blunted by its own leadership, the crisis for Gairy was relieved and he was soon building a compromise between himself, the disaffected elements of the local bourgeoisie and the Churches. 'Gifts' were received from Britain and substantial loans from the governments of Jamaica, Trinidad and Guyana for Gairy's successful restitution. The Churches were placated with air-time on the radio station and a large illuminated cross on the crest behind St George's. The Grenadian masses had suffered their second monumental sell-out, twenty-three years after 'Sky Red', and watched the leadership that had betrayed them rewarded by Gairy with an appointment to the 'Senate', a cosmetic upper house that was a part of his pseudo-democratic camouflage.[16]

Towards the Revolutionary solution: 1974–79

While Gairy attempted to retrieve his prestige through his empty assertions that Grenada was now truly an 'independent' nation, 'in spite of the wicked malicious, obstructive and destructive efforts of the small noise-making, self-publicizing minority', the militants of the New Jewel Movement studied the events of the previous months as a salutary lesson. They plunged their roots deeper and deeper into the organizations of the village communities and the working class, making more profound their links with the masses and bringing real and concrete benefits as they campaigned for 'not just another society, but a just society'. They established pre-primary schools, 'freedom schools', house repair schemes, a clandestine network of village assemblies and emergent mass organizations of students, youth and women. Whenever workers or small farmers were campaigning and organizing against the abuses of Gairyism, the NJM was there, leading the struggles. A new type of party militant emerged from the guts of the people, and in particular women began to play a crucial role in what had become by this time an anti-fascist struggle. Scotilda Noel, from Birch Grove in St Andrew's, became an example of the new Grenadian woman that was being steeled through this period. Her comrade-founder of the National Women's Organization, Phyllis Coard, recounts her contribution:

> Scotty came from a very loving and close family in Birch Grove. After getting married she emigrated to England, where she had six children. In England she saw capitalism and imperialism at very close hand, also actually experiencing the insults of racism. This was enough to tell her clearly that such a system and such a society could never work for the benefit of the ordinary and working people.
>
> When she came home to Grenada she joined the party and was very active in organizing the small farmers, and the women in particular, in the banana-growing area of Birch Grove. She later became, after the Revolution, a founding member of the Agricul- tural and General Workers' Union. She began a Party Support Group in the village and was also one of the seven pioneers who began the National Women's Organization.
>
> At that time in Birch Grove, she had to confront the full force of Gairyism, with all its violence and brutality. The area was very much dominated by the wickedness and misdeeds of Inspector Innocent Belmar, one of the most unscrupulous of Gairy's hench- men.
>
> Even after her husband died, tragically early, through cancer, she carried on mobilizing and organizing right up to the Revolution and after, and it was only her own death by car accident on 2 November 1979, that managed to stop her ceaseless and selfless activity on behalf of the Grenadian people.[17]

Gairy's growing fascist dimension now took on an external aspect with his close ties with the ruling régimes of Chile, Haiti and South Korea. He sent his police officers to train in Chile, welcomed the prison ship *Esmeralda* into Grenadian waters and received arms for his Green Beasts from Pinochet. He intrigued, too, to sell Grenada's offshore fishing rights to the South Korean Government — a move thwarted by the NJM's mobilization of Grenadian fishermen. Whenever he moved, the 'Jewel' were there to expose him, to oppose and tackle him, to organize against his violence and fraudulence and pour scorn upon his obscurantism and 'ufology'. The growing ideological maturity, stamina and political toughness of the party cadres of the mid and late 1970s is exemplified in the life and death of Alister Strachan, who was murdered by Gairy's police on 19 June, 1977. He had dived into the sea to escape from the dictator's gunmen after the break-up of an NJM meeting in the Market Square which had been called to coincide with a meeting of the Organization of American States in Grenada, at which the featured guest was Cyrus Vance, President Carter's chief foreign affairs spokesman and Secretary of State. The guns kept shooting at Alister as he swam out to sea; later his corpse was washed ashore. His childhood friend, Edwin Frank, now a newscaster on Radio Free Grenada, tells his story:

Alister was born in the sugar cane area of Calivigny. I remember that he was very skilful at all those games we associate with childhood. We used to play marbles together, fly kites together, climb trees and play in the cane-fields. He was a good cricketer and captained Woburn School team, but he also played football and basketball and was a strong swimmer, although he mastered that later in his childhood. But more than anything, people knew him as a great runner. At school he was very friendly with everyone, the teachers liked him — and the girls certainly did, too.

He first attended St Geoge's Methodist School and later, when the new school was built, Woburn. He loved school and studying, particularly history and mathematics, but it was after he left school that he first realized how difficult it was to be living in our country during those years. Just to get a job was one of the hardest tasks for a young man. Many times he used to tell me about going around day after day looking for work, and the answer was always the same. Then he finally found something as a mechanic, but even then he couldn't take the exploitation: 'You working, working and nothing coming!' he used to say, and would get very angry and frustrated with that system of life. But he always loved the land, just like his father and mother. He was ardent for the land and always helped them, and also grew some lettuce and cabbage for himself. The funds he got from selling that kept him alive during those terrible days.

Even while he was doing that, he was all the time developing his knowledge and consciousness that made him what he was. He borrowed a lot of books from some of the militant comrades of those times, and he always read, read, read. He was one of the few people that you could have heard speaking about the African struggles. He knew a lot about what was happening in Angola, about the struggle in Mozambique and also the war in Vietnam — and the situations in Central America and Chile. He told us all about them. Now, looking back, I can understand how correct he was. I also remember back to 1976 and his angry reaction to the Soweto massacre of the South African schoolchildren. He felt deeply for anyone struggling for freedom, particularly the guerrillas and those who gave up everything to fight in the bush.

He used to stand in his back garden and I used to stand in mine, and we always took a rest together. He was the one who really opened the way for me. I was more interested in studying school work in those times, but it was Alister who told me about the wider things around us. He used to rap on the block to all the local youth and try to open their eyes too.

In his political work he was always out advertising meetings of the NJM and constantly campaigning. He painted a lot of slogans right throughout the south of Grenada, and through endless hours of the night he would be going from wall to wall with his paint and brush. He also sold and distributed the party paper on a weekly basis, but he had to be very careful, and he tried to keep it underground. He painted jerseys for people too — I remember one he painted for African Liberation Day in 1976 or 1977. He was a *real* activist, always mobilizing, always on the move, on the go all the time, *always* going — particularly during the last few months of his life when the police were after him and always victimizing him.

I remember him mobilizing right up to his death, and giving out pamphlets for that very Market Square meeting where he was killed. There was an important OAS meeting here at the time, and the comrades really wanted to expose Gairy internationally for what he was. I remember that day, although I was studying for an economics exam which I had the next day, so I didn't go to the Market Square myself. But we had lunch together before he left, corned beef and biscuits under the mango tree, and he left his stereo tape recorder with me and told he'd see me later.

Of course, Gairy's men intervened and broke up the meeting, even though it was peaceful. They started shooting, and then they saw Alister. They always had an eye on him and were trying to catch up with him, so they chased him down to the Esplanade where he dived into the sea somewhere behind the police station there. People were scampering everywhere and running, and while this was happening the police started shooting at him, just taking pot-shots while he swam out and kept diving down. It was real chaos all about, real haywire as many people later told me, and very few people really understood what was happening, they couldn't get an overall picture of the scene. It was only later, when people began to recollect together, that they managed to put the pieces together and realize what had actually happened. It was three days later, and I hadn't seen Alister all that time, when I was working in my garden and I heard on the radio about a man being washed ashore on some beach. So I called his mother, and she went down to see the body — only to realize that it was her own son. Then everybody seemed to remember how it happened, how he had been swimming in the sea away from the shots.

His death made the youths and students realize more and more what was happening to them, even though many were very active and conscious already. But it boosted their consciousness even more about the violence, the repression and Gairy's complete lack of respect and feeling for the people. It made them more determined and brought out more of them to be directly involved in the movement.

In terms of his commitment to the struggle he was a real example. Towards the end of his life it was clear that the continuous harrassment and hounding by the police was affecting him, but he never gave way and never gave up struggling, mobilizing. He always said, 'that day will come, that Revolution will come!' — every day he said that, 'the day of Liberation is coming!' And he was right.[18]

Gairy continued to use Parliament and the Westminster system as a cover of his murderous repression. His cynical commentary on the NJM: 'With a transparent lust for power, they favour bullets while we adhere to ballots', was in reality a confession of his own strategy — to rig ballots while he fired bullets. Mysterious disappearances also became a part of his repertoire. Those who disappeared were political opponents of Gairy, sometimes, like Inspector Iri Bishop of Carriacou, they were honest people who simply disapproved of his brutality and sometimes, like the four young men of Six Roads village, Carriacou, who tended their goats on the small uninhabited Frigate Island, they simply got in the way when he needed to appropriate animals for his own use. Four years after these events, Jacob Ross, a young Grenadian poet, wrote the following:

REQUIEM FOR FIVE

For Iri Bishop and the four who disappeared on Frigate Island, because they dared to say 'No'

We did not find them
    beneath
The mounds of sand
The careful search
Of earth and grass
Revealed no scars or
How death had come to pass.

We looked between the tortured roots of trees
Found nothing in the twisting folds of wind
Nothing, but the skeleton of leaves
    stuck between
    the hollowed teeth of rocks.

The land has left no trace
The lipless wind no clue
The sun's unsheathed eye
— too furious and distant
To let these secrets through.

We do not know
    If
Perhaps the restless tongue of waves
Have repeated these things through the years
Have echoed them on every shore
— the time and nature of the crime.

We do not know
The seagulls

May have scribbled it with rippling wings
Upon the pages of the wind
What they in silent rage had seen.

We do not know
    To
Crack these elemental codes
What may be written with the ink of the sea
By the blood-ringed fingers of sea weeds
Upon our many beaches.

We do not know
    Where
Their bodies lie
If coffined between corals
With a funeral of coloured fish
Or the octopus' slow procession
    Or if
They have fed the flesh of sharks.

We do not know
    Though
Oftentimes we think we hear
When moon is low and night less dark
Through the suck and surge of quiet tides
In syllables of sea on sand
The slow notes of a mournful song

IRI BISHOP'S THERE, LIES OVER THERE
CRIED OVER THERE, DIED OVER THERE
THE FOUR YOUTHS, HERE, CRIED OVER HERE
DIED OVER HERE, LIE OVER HERE

Sometimes we think . . .

We do not know.

During the 1976 Elections the NJM formed a tactical alliance
with the other opposition elements, the GNP and also the

United People's Party, a small grouping representing a particularly aggressive arm of the local commercial class which had split
with Gairy. With the help of wholesale lying and intimidation of
the voters, plain electoral fraud (there were five thousand false
names on the electoral register) and monopolization of the
national media with the opposition unable even to use public
address systems, Gairy precariously managed to take the election, and the three elected NJM members became the leaders of
the opposition, thus providing them with a regular national
platform — despite the fact that Whiteman was soon ejected for
making remarks unfavourable to Gairy in a parliamentary
debate.

Gairy's union machine was also, like his parliamentary
apparatus, becoming more and more riddled with absurdity and
fraud, while the NJM was growing in strength and credibility
within the urban unions, particularly the Commercial and
Industrial Workers' Union and the Technical and Allied Workers' Union. Gairy's 'pappyshow' union actually forced more
people out of work than found jobs for them, and formed yet
another layer of his repressive apparatus. As a woman road
worker declared:

> Gairy have a union and we all have to join. Them used to take up we
> money, and we never saw that money at all again. Everybody must
> pay something of their pay. If you earning five dollars a week then
> the union take out a dollar fifty. I used to work for eighteen dollars a
> fortnight and they used to take three dollar fifty for the union. I
> never see no benefits from this union up to now, and I worked from
> January 1960 up to the overthrow. I never get anything for what I
> pay, I never get a cent back, not for sick pay, not for unemploy-
> ment, not for anything. They never help us when we were out of
> work, it was simply money wasted that was never any benefit to
> you. We never knew where the money go and we struggling all the
> time with we children to pay school and to buy books. If you ent
> join the union, you ent get work, and if you don't pay, even if you
> don't work, you still have to get the money to pay for it. And then
> you pay and you still ent getting work! In the end I couldn't pay the
> union card, so I stop work and try to find other work like washing
> clothes for people.[19]

The dictator's anti-worker laws and fostering of a compliant
leadership in the major unions gave him a direct control over

industrial relations. He could hire and fire on behalf of almost any firm:

> All we got with Gairy was victimization. He never listened to the workers. He was never interested in what the poor people had to say, he was only for the rich. He never asked the workers for their opinions. If we spoke out, that was that! I was working in Kirpalani's in those days and a few of us workers were speaking out about the state of things in the country. So as the business change hands, Gairy call all the workers to a meeting at Progress House. One of the workers that was for him had brought the news to him. So he told us, the ones that had spoken out, that we would not be employed in the company again. He put us right out of work, even though the management knew we were good workers and wanted us to work there still! It was only after he was overthrown that I found a job again, for he would never let me work again in Grenada while he was still the government.[20]

Such hegemonic industrial power was challenged in late 1978, by the newly-formed Bank and General Workers' Union, led by NJM stalwart, Vincent Noel. When the Barclays Bank workers demanded union recognition and an end to the insulting racist attitude of their employers during both working hours and wage negotiations, Gairy joined hands with Barclays to frustrate recognition and jailed Noel. The Barclays Bank workers' strike in February and March 1979 brought substantial support from the middle and commercial classes for the NJM and Gairy was clearly becoming more and more desperate. By 10 March, word had come down to the NJM leaders from progressive elements in the police force that Gairy was about to arrest them and had made ready subterranean prison cells for them. They went into hiding. On 12 March Gairy left the state, stopping in Barbados to consult with American Ambassador, Frank Ortiz, leaving instructions to his forces to carry out the assassination of the six major NJM figures. On 13 March, at dawn, fifty NJM comrades, the genesis of the People's Revolutionary Army, struck against the main barracks of the Green Beast army at Trueblue and, having scattered the troops, continued to take the Radio Station at Morne Rouge, broadcasting to the Grenadian people to support the insurrection, take up arms and ensure that every police station in the state surrendered. By sunset, with people out cheering in their thousands with cutlassess, sticks, knives and old firearms or anything they could muster, with the police stations in their hands and Gairy's ministers and hoodlums under lock and key, the first revolution in the English-speaking Caribbean was a day old and a new beginning had opened wide for the Grenadian people:

> The soldiers of Justice all ready to fight
> Worked smooth and efficiently all through the night.
> While thousands were home sleeping deep in their bed
> Freedom fighters rendered their blood to be shed.
> With the grace of the masses and the cry of the poor
> The guns of the downpressed we saw victory's door.

> *The people call it Freedom Day*
> *Old people say Freedom Day*
> *Young people say Freedom Day*
> *I and I say Freedom Day*
> *The NJM say Freedom Day*
> *The rastaman say Freedom Day*
> *The PRA say Freedom Day*
> *We going with Freedom Day —*
> *For Justice, Equality, Equal Opportunity*
> *For evermore Grenadians say Freedom Day!* [21]

But with this beginning came other beginnings. For as Bishop addressed a joyous people and Gairy raged in disbelief in the USA (the final sanctuary for deposed tyrants, for Somoza of Nicaragua and the Shah of Iran, too, in the same year), organized imperialist destabilization with all its most advanced and tested methods was already stirring itself into mobilization against the people's victory.

PART 2: COME THE REVOLUTION, COME DESTABILIZATION

We think of the history of US Imperialism. We think of the days when the gunboats ruled the world; when you landed marines in someone else's country: Arbenz in Guatemala in 1954, Dominican Republic in 1965 and dozens of other examples. We think of the occupations and the annexations of other people's territories, particularly in our region, in Latin America and the Caribbean. We think of the assassinations of Sandino the patriot of Nicaragua, of Allende the hero of Chile, of so many other martyrs of this region who had to die at the hands of imperialism.

We think of the scientific way in which they have evolved a new concept which they have called 'destabilization': a concept aimed at creating political violence, economic sabotage; a concept which when it fails, eventually leads to terrorism. We think of the attempts to use local opportunists and counter-revolutionaries — people who try to build a popular base, people who fail in building that popular base, and people who as a result of having failed to fool the masses then turn to the last weapon they have in desperation: the weapons of open, naked, brutal and vulgar terror — having given up all hope of winning the masses, these people now turn their revenge on the masses.

Maurice Bishop: radio address on the night of the fatal counter-revolutionary bombing at Queen's Park, 19 June 1980

FROM THE outset of revolutionary power in 1979, the People's Revolutionary Government began a systematic education of their people about the dangers and the causes of destabilization. The mass mobilization of the people through popular organizations such as the National Women's Organization and the National Youth Organization, plus the gradual development of parish and zonal democratic structures like the Parish Councils and the Workers' Parish Councils, laid the organizational base for this mass education. One month after the Revolution, Prime Minister Bishop, in a speech which included the now celebrated phrase that Grenada 'is not in anybody's backyard', pointed to the lessons that Grenadians must learn from the attempts then being made to destabilize and block the popular advances being made in Jamaica by the Michael Manley Government. He pointed to the terrifying level of propaganda destabilization being produced through the local, regional and international media and to the damage consequently being done to the Jamaican economy and tourist trade. He also emphasized that what had happened in 1975 and 1976 in Jamaica 'could soon begin to happen in our country'.

Three weeks later, on the night of 6 May, arsonists burned down two buildings crucially connected to the Grenadian tourist industry: the Grenada International Travel Agency in St George's and a tourist cottage near the Grande Anse Beach. The Prime Minister responded with a national radio address which was afterwards printed and circulated around the country under the title: *Organize to fight Destabilization!*. The Orange Lane fire of May 1976 in Jamaica, and the horrific fire at the Eventide Old People's Home which followed, when one hundred and fifty aged citizens were burned to death, had also been grim warnings to Grenada. The Grenadian people were being made aware of the menace that now confronted them, and 'destabilization' became the latest addition to the lexicon of the Revolution and the watchword for greater and greater vigilance. It was defined and explained by Bishop in these terms:

> Sisters and brothers, destabilization is the name given to the most recently developed (or newest) method of controlling and exploiting the lives and resources of a country and its people by a bigger and more powerful country through bullying, intimidation and violence. In the old days, such countries—the colonialist and imperialist powers — sent in gunboats or marines to take over directly the country by sheer force. Later on mercenaries were often used in place of soldiers, navy and marines.
>
> Today, more and more the new weapon and the new menace is destabilization. This method was used against a number of Caribbean and Third World countries in the 1960s, and also against Jamaica and Guyana in the 1970s. Now, as was predicted, it has come to Grenada.

What was being made clear was that Grenada was facing a new kind of threat, a threat which must be known and understood in all its forms by the Grenadian people if their revolution was to survive. It was not the blatant caricature of colonial gunboats on the horizon anymore. Imperialism had moved onto a new phase with novel and more subtle methods to be applied from an almost limitless budget and it was imperative that the people be educated and equipped to be able to identify and fight it.

Mercenary Threats and Military Destabilization

During the centuries of colonial domination in the Caribbean, the concept of destabilization was unknown and uninvented because it was unnecessary. The colonial powers kept standing military forces in their colonies and could always summon more from other neighbouring colonies to deal with rebellion. When Julien Fedon led his 1795 insurrection in Grenada, the British quickly sought to ship in more troops from their other Caribbean possessions to support their beleaguered garrison in St George's, and also reinforced these with further forces sent by the governor of the neighbouring Spanish colony of Trinidad. Echoes of this direct and vulgar tactic still resound in the Caribbean, for example, the 1980 revolt in Union Island (one of the Grenadians forming a part of the state of St Vincent and the Grenadines) was only suppressed when the threatened Cato Government called in military help from Barbados, acting the part of the imperialist policeman of the Eastern Caribbean. However, the USA, with a history over the last century of 135 direct military interventions in the Caribbean and Latin America, including those in Guatemala in 1954 and the Dominican Republic in 1965, has come to represent even to the erstwhile British colonial territories, the most formidable threat to progressive and independent government. But the expulsion of the US-backed counter-revolutionary force of Cuban exiles at Playa Giron in 1961, showed that a vigilant and organized people could respond effectively and decisively.

Military destabilization of small island states like Grenada has more recently become a promising industry for mercenaries. The invasion of the Comores Islands in the Indian Ocean in 1977 by a group of mercenaries led by the international murderer Bob Denard, led to the expulsion of a progressive government there.

This model was followed in the abortive mercenary attempt to invade the Seychelles Islands in December 1981 and oust the government of Albert René. The South African-led adventure was smashed at the Seychelles International Airport by a vigilant popular army. Thus, states like Grenada with their hundreds of beaches, have become particularly vulnerable; a fact that was not lost upon the US State Department. For having refused the People's Revolutionary Government's request for Gairy's extradition to face charges of murder and multiple fraud, the US Government allowed him to begin to recruit a mercenary force to attack Grenada. In April 1979, the ex-dictator's plotting came to light when a letter to him from Frank Mabri, a notorious mercenary recruiter, was intercepted. Right up to the present time, the US Government allows the training of mercenaries in Florida and Georgia, plus the free circulation of their glossy magazine *Soldier of Fortune*. These men are publicly on record in declaring that their eventual destinations are Cuba, Nicaragua and Grenada. In April 1981, ten mercenaries were arrested in the USA just as they were about to embark on a mercenary invasion of Dominica. This was later revealed to be just the first step of a Caribbean operation which would eventually have led them to a landing in Grenada, their principal target. The commander of this operation was one Michael Perdue.

On 21 May 1981 *The Toronto Globe and Mail* newspaper published an interview with James McQuirter, the Grand Wizard of the Canadian Knights of the Ku Klux Klan, and Donald Andrews, former head of the racist Western Guard. They admitted that Perdue had often discussed with them his dream of controlling a Caribbean island for a base of operations. After the 1979 Revolution, Grenada had become a favourite candidate, as Perdue harboured a further fantasy of 'toppling a revolutionary government'. He had contacted Gairy after the latter's flight to the US in 1979, but the two differed over what was to be the best strategy for a mercenary attack. Perdue preferred sending armed mercenaries directly by boat, but the Gairy plan was for them·to enter the country posing as tourists and then to seize weapons from the police and the People's Revolutionary Army. Finally, the conspirators flew to Dominica on the pretence of establishing a small business which would become a front for the future assault on Grenada. The first 'mission' to Dominica was made in November 1979 by a man called 'Mr P', who was in fact a Western Guard member who had been active in several organized racist incidents in Toronto in the 1970s, including the painting of swastikas on the city's synagogues.[22]

This resorting to mercenaries, however, has not prevented or been any kind of substitute for the continuation of repeated US provocations in the Eastern Caribbean through military manoeuvres and shows of force. Shortly after the Revolution, the US Government was contemplating the creation of a naval quarantine of Grenada. This was not applied, but led directly to the 'Solid Shield '80' manoeuvres, which had the objective of instilling fear and intimidation into the hearts of the Cuban and Grenadian people in particular, or any of the oppressed masses of the Caribbean who were looking towards the Cuban or Grenadian Revolutions for their inspiration.

In this way mercenary activity has been complemented by the sabre-rattling of the US Government, which by August 1981 was under the openly belligerent control of Ronald Reagan, who in his election speeches was fond of calling Cuba, Grenada and Nicaragua mere 'temporary obstacles' to US hegemony in the region. His first initiative, called 'Ocean Venture '81', deployed over 120,000 troops, 250 warships and 1,000 aircraft at Vieques Island near Puerto Rico. The provocation was code-named 'Amber and the Amberines'.[23] It was, of course, an uncanny coincidence that Grenada's full national name is 'Grenada and the Grenadines', and that Amber is the name of a land area very near to the site of the new international airport being built at Point Salines in Grenada. This open dress rehearsal for an invasion of Grenada was conducted by US Rangers over the mountainous terrain of Vieques, which is very similar in its geographical features to Grenada. Before this the paratroopers flew during the night from Norton Air Base, California, to Florida, covering the same distance as from their Wilmington Base to Grenada. The objective was to capture 'Amber', hold US-style elections and install a 'government friendly to America', keeping troops occupying the island until the elections were over. The manoeuvres were conducted with support from Britain and Holland — these two powers, together with the US, being the last colonial powers in the Caribbean.

The clichés behind the mock invasion were transparently obvious. 'Amber' was supported by 'Orange' (Cuba), which in turn was supported by 'Red' (the Soviet Union). Rear Admiral

McKenzie, who commanded the operation, announced at the manoeuvres' press conference that he considered Grenada, Nicaragua and Cuba as 'one country', and that the reason for the attack on 'Amber' was that its government was 'exporting terrorist activities to the neighbouring islands'. He all but admitted that the real target of the mock assault was Grenada by announcing that the 'objective' was an 'island' with a 2,000-man army. The practice invasion was purportedly to 'rescue twenty US citizens held hostage there after negotiations with the Amber Government had broken down', and after the 'elections' it would be assured that the new government 'would be favourable to the way of life we espouse'. All this, declared the Rear Admiral, was to 'give an example of one facet of US capabilities to respond in the Caribbean Basin'.[24]

Three months later, in November 1981, the US forces in the Caribbean commenced the 'Red X 183' manoeuvres, which followed a two-day meeting of military chiefs from Latin America and the Caribbean — including Jamaica (since October 1981 under the control of the US-inspired Seaga Government), Barbados and Trinidad — with the Pentagon, examining methods of dealing with any popular or revolutionary movement in the region. The 'Red X 183' manoeuvres again involved the use of thousands of US troops and dozens of planes and warships, and coincided with military exercises on the Honduras–Nicaragua border, as well as with a violent verbal attack against Cuba by Alexander Haig, the Secretary of State in Washington, the breaking of relations between Jamaica and Cuba by Seaga, and the presence in and around the Eastern Caribbean of the giant, nuclear-powered aircraft carrier, USS *Eisenhower* — which was making a 'goodwill' visit to Barbados and launching its planes in low-flying bravado exhibitions off the coast of that island.[25]

In May 1982, Grenada's air traffic controllers received a message from Piarco Airport in Trinidad, informing them with three hours' notice that an area in the Caribbean Sea just forty or fifty miles off the coast of Grenada, had been designated as 'manoeuvres area'. The Trinidad air traffic controllers were merely passing on a message that had been received from the Washington Federal Aviation Administration Air Traffic Control System Command Centre, and the consequence was that suddenly the Eastern Caribbean nations from Dominica down to Trinidad, had lost control over their own air space. As a result, regular flights between Trinidad and Grenada were cancelled, although the regional airline, LIAT, did not receive official notification until hours later — and then their pilots found themselves compelled to use visual means for take-off and landing.

This was overt US backyardism, manifesting a total contempt for the Caribbean people and an insult to all nations in the region, whether or not they were friendly to the Reagan Administration. Typically it was only the Government of Grenada that protested against the US armed trespass. To Grenada it was another 'classic example', in Bishop's words, 'of the arrogance, contempt and insensitivity of the US administration of Ronald Reagan', an arrogance that is a constant threat continuing day by day in the Caribbean.

Terrorist Destabilization

Destabilization soon took the form of organizing local Grenadian counter-revolutionaries to use terrorist measures in attempts to scare the population and force them to lose confidence in the revolutionary leadership. In November 1979 the 'De Raveniere Plot' was unmasked shortly before it was to be implemented, and ex-police corporal Wilton de Raveniere admitted his connexions with other counter-revolutionary elements, both inside and outside the island. When his home was searched, the evidence was plain to see: a map of Grenada with strategic positions marked, a notebook which, amongst other coded notes of contacts contained the words: 'St George's was burnt once and it could be done again', some sophisticated communications equipment and quantities of arms, ammunition and explosive devices. De Raveniere later admitted: 'We were going to wait for American boats with mercenaries and extra arms aboard to land at three different points in the island early the next morning, to make the final move.'

Upon further investigations, De Raveniere was found to be linked to other disaffected elements from various backgrounds who were united in a counter-revolutionary desire. Also involved were Winston Whyte, who in Gairy's time had formed the United People's Party, representing the interests of a section of the more aggressive local capitalist class, some pseudo-rastafarians who had hoped the Revolution would satisfy their

dreams of large-scale marijuana trafficking, and a politically
ambitious Grenadian academic teaching at Howard University,
Washington, Stanley Cyrus. Cyrus and his chief henchman,
James Herry, soon became the darlings of anti-Grenada elements in the Caribbean media network, particularly to radio
stations like Radio Trinidad and Radio Antilles, and were ready
and eager to act as catalysts to promote any terrorist outrage
against the Grenada Revolution.

Then, in Spring 1980, 'The Budhlall Gang', led by brothers
Kenneth and Kennedy Budhlall who had also been associates of
De Raveniere, attempted to organize some youths in the Tivoli
area of St Patrick's Parish, many of them rastafarians, against the
People's Revolutionary Government (PRG). They seized a
large estate at River Antoine with bloated ultra-left rhetoric
and, claiming to be more revolutionary than the Revolution,
began to organize the mass cultivation of marijuana. At a
public demonstration they called for the violent overthrow of
the government. They also formulated plans aimed at assassin-
ating the leadership and attacking two major military camps —
Fort Rupert and the Grand Etang Fort — synchronizing their
plans with the appearance of a mysterious helicopter over
Grenada's only airport.

In both of these cases, the vigilance of the people and the
People's Revolutionary Army (PRA), prevented the actual
accomplishment of the climax of counter-revolution but, on 19
June 1980, imperialist destabilization wrought terror and death
in Grenada. At a rally to celebrate Heroes' Day, a sophisticated
and powerful time-bomb was detonated under the grandstand
in Queen's Park, close to where the entire revolutionary leadership was sitting. The blast missed its main target, but caused the
death of three young women and injury to over ninety more
people. The next day, twenty thousand indignant Grenadians
took to the streets in a massive march of protest and defiance,
and the Flying Turkey later sang of the murderous force and
consequence of destabilization:

> Turn them into robots, puppets on a string,
> They kill their own sisters
> And they don't care a thing.
> Imperialism on that afternoon
> Raised its cruel hands
> And innocent blood get shed,

And now Bernadette, Laurice and Laureen
are all dead.

Security forces soon discovered the source of the weapon, and
later the same day a treacherous PRA soldier, one Strachan
Phillip, was killed after opening fire on the police, who had
traced the cause of the explosion to his house. This turned out to
be an arsenal of automatic weapons, harbouring as well the same
kind of detonating device used to set off the murderous bomb.
Cyrus, predictably speaking over Radio Antilles, referred to
Phillip as a 'hero', and evidence soon linked him as a part of the
organization responsible for the assassination attempt, along
with the Budhlalls. This was confirmed a week later when a
saboteur with an identical device — who was a protégé of the
Budhlalls — blew himself up while attempting to lay a charge in
Belmont, St George's.

Then, on the night of 17 November 1980, terrorist destabilizers struck again. Four young men — Stephen Lalsee, Andrew
Courtney, Donald Stanislaus and his brother Dennis, who was
on holiday in Grenada from England and was due to return the
next day — were gunned down in St Patrick's Parish as they
stepped from their car after stopping to help what they thought
was another motorist in trouble. The same night the murderers
continued their work, shooting and mutilating a young militiaman, Evan Charles, who was on duty at his camp at Mount
Rose. The nation rose as one in mass anger at these acts. The
people recognized the hideous face of counter-revolution and
sensed the true meaning of destabilization. Such violence had
been unknown in Grenada since the brutalities of Gairy's
Mongoose Gang had been ended by the revolutionary dawn of
13 March and the people were stunned that such events could
ever happen again. Young Evon Charles, called 'Quiety' by his
friends because of his taciturnity, had been found with four
bullets in his body and his face slashed, his eyes cut out and his
chest carved repeatedly with a bayonet. Nineteen bullets were
embedded in Stephen Lalsee's body.

In response to the murder of their young comrades, particu-
larly Lalsee who was a student at the Institute of Further
Education, and Courtney, who was still studying at McDonald
College, Sauteurs, over a thousand secondary school children
marched through the streets of St George's on the following
Thursday, chanting, 'If they play with fire, revolutionary fire

go burn them!' and carrying a huge banner declaring: 'Revolution has no room for terrorists — Join the Militia now and fight terrorism!' Pupils of many schools throughout the nation issued statements of protest. The girls of St Joseph's Convent declared: 'Let us show these local terrorists and the outside world that we will fight to our last drop of blood!' and the boys of the Grenada Boys' Secondary School added: 'We extend our sincere and profound sympathy to the families of the lost ones. Their blood will not flow in vain, for we will join our new revolutionary cadets and militia to defend our brothers.' From the sister island of Carriacou the students of Bishop's College called out across the sea: 'Imperialism has struck again, but social justice for our people will go forward ever, backward never!'[26] It was clear that the terrorists had provoked nothing but greater determination amongst the people they had sought to intimidate, and deeper and deeper seams of revolutionary will had been uncovered to intensify the struggle against destabilization.

In all these cases, imperialism had used local stooges and criminal elements to operate on its behalf, and thus avoid at this juncture direct external aggression. It could then argue that Grenadians themselves were unhappy with their own revolution, and that it had no responsibility for any acts of resistance. Yet the hidden hand of imperialism was always there, as Bishop made clear during his Heroes' Day address exactly one year after the fatal Queen's Park bombing:

> We have several different forms and shapes and faces and figures. They don't come simply in black or in brown or in white. They don't simply come in forms of fatness or shortness or roundness. They come in all kinds of shapes and sizes and we have to be conscious of all the different faces, sizes, colours.

Destabilization through Backward Trade Union Leadership

In the same speech, the Prime Minister warned of destabilization at work within the Grenadian trade union bureaucracy and the 'corrupt, opportunist trade union leaders'. He continued: 'that is one of the most popular categories of the CIA for counter-revolution.' Under the Gairy dictatorship such elements had continually sold out their members and Gairy himself could always rely upon them to head off any real struggle emerging from the mass of the workers. In 1974, the betrayal by sections of the leadership of the Seamen and Waterfront Workers Union that had been associated with the forerunner of the American Institute of Free Labor Development, at that very moment when the Dockworkers' strike was facing Gairy with complete defeat, had swung the advantage right back to the dictator and divided the most militant section of the nation's small working class. The CIA, directly through its sub-agency, the AIFLD, had its trainees in other trade union bureaucracies, particularly among leading officials of the Technical and Allied Workers' Union. In October 1979 one of these was implicated in the De Raveniere Plot, and was inciting workers in the Grenada Electicity Company (GRENLEC), to strike and cut off current to the entire country to create the chaos necessary for the success of the intended mercenary invasion. Another local graduate of the AIFLD attempted to foment dissatisfaction when a Cuban boat arrived at the docks in St George's, full of cement which was a gift to the Government of Grenada. One of the dockers present remembered that 'this CIA man, say we shouldn't unload the stern hatch because the hole too small. Then Comrade Strachan the Minister, come and tell we that the cement was free, but we should make a price for whatever we want to take out the cement. So the CIA man say he not making any price and just walk away. So the men say they wouldn't do it.'[27] Similarly, when a cargo of free milk arrived from Europe in December 1980 with a stipulation that, as a gift, it should be unloaded free of charge, destabilizing elements in the leadership of the Seamen and Waterfront Workers' Union again urged the dockworkers to strike, despite clear explanations by government representatives that unless the milk was unloaded by unpaid labour it would be forfeit. In the event, members of the Women's National Organization worked alongside a number of dockers to unload the milk for pre-Christmas distribution.

During the period leading up to the second anniversary of the Revolution on 13 March 1982, the leaders of the Public Workers' Union, the Grenada Union of Teachers and the Technical and Allied Workers' Union called a 'sick-out' while negotiations were continuing on the Government's 36 per cent pay increase, offered over three years in response to the unions' demand for 70 per cent. The PRG, indeed, upholds the right of *all* workers, including those working for the Government or for

State enterprises, to take industrial action, and agricultural workers on government estates and workers at the Central Water Commission have done so. Yet this action of the white-collar unions was generally seen by the mass of the people as premature, unreasonable and sectarian in the context of a youthful revolution striving to elevate the standard of living for *all* its population, and in particular for the low-paid agricultural workers who, with the continuing decline in world market prices for their products, could not hope for anything like a similar increase in salary.

There was a genuine and militant outrage against the strikers and, in Sauteurs and River Sallee in St Patrick's Parish, in St John's and in St George's, demonstrators took to the streets. Schoolchildren carried placards calling the teachers to 'Teach the Youth' and, in St John's, a placard put the people's position squarely: 'If you love Grenada *work* to build Grenada. Then the money must come!' Slogans appeared on walls, 'Down with CIA trade unions!' and many people made their positions absolutely clear to journalists of *The Free West Indian*. Claris Smith of Gouyave declared: 'I found it very stupid. They should have thought of the country and the children. Things not only hard for civil servants, it's hard for everybody, including the Government.' Marcelle Commissiong, also from Gouyave, added: 'I find they could have waited for a much longer time to make such demands on a poor country as ours. The country really just start. They could have pushed for money later. It's clear they trying to embarrass the Revo.' A worker in the Ministry of Education, Patricia Ogilvie, was quite firm why she came in to work: 'It's true that an increase is needed, but the country is poor and the union leaders and some members must see this reasoning and check themselves. Any raise in pay must be the consequence of a rise in production.' Finally, Norris Perrotte of Mount Granby put the majority view quite clearly, and demonstrated how much the people were learning: 'Counter-revolution comes in all forms, but people must be able to recognize it when they see it. Even those who are blind could recognize that the 70 per cent just ent there! Their sick-out is totally irresponsible. The Revo is a baby of two years. Gairy was there for twenty-five years and never did anything that compares with the last two years. These union leaders appear to have short memories.'[28]

Against this massive public pressure, the sick-out failed and an agreement was finally reached some weeks later. But the incident was a clear pointer to many of the people that the trade unions can be manipulated to play a backward role, particularly in a situation when workers' unity is necessary to support a workers' government intent on building a workers' state. Many Grenadian workers also remembered 1974, when in spite of the many voices inside the Civil Service Association (as the Public Workers' Union was then called) raised in support of the striking dockers, the union leaders had manoeuvred a vote against such a move by suddenly unionizing a large number of daily-paid workers who were inexperienced in trade union affairs, and who voted according to the instructions of the union leadership.

This same retrogressive attitude continued when, during the following October, the Public Workers' Union Executive invited an associate of Stanley Cyrus, a Grenadian who was at the time a lecturer of the University of the West Indies, Barbados Campus, to deliver the feature address at their 1981 Special General Meeting. The speaker attacked the People's Revolutionary Government with a number of wild assertions, including an accusation that the standard of education in Grenada was falling, even though there was a clear increase in examination successes that year throughout the nation. This was another warning to Grenadians that some sections of the trade union leadership were still playing their old frightened, anti-worker role, and was certainly one of the stimuli which led rank-and-file public workers over the following year to fight resolutely to democratize their union.[29]

Destabilization by the Multinationals

The People's Revolutionary Government is very conscious of the massive power that the multinational corporations have to control and destabilize the economy of a small island state like Grenada that is determined to build its economic independence. The Geest banana monopoly, for example, threw the Windward Islands, including Grenada, into real anxiety, when, after Hurricane Allen of 1980, it began to buy its bananas from Central America — and then said, after production was normalizing again in the Windwards, that they had resolved to continue to buy Central American bananas rather than those of the Windwards because 'the British housewife' preferred the non-speckled Central American variety. Therefore, instructed Geest, Windward Islands' bananas must look as well as taste like their cousins in Colombia and Costa Rica.

In this type of context the only answer was to seek an economic policy that demonopolized the markets and diversified production. Finance Minister Coard commented in an interview as early as July 1979:

> For us the most important aspect in building an economically independent country (which is the only way that you can truly say that you are politically independent) is the method of diversification — in all ways, in all aspects. First, diversification of agricultural production, secondly diversification of the markets that we sell these products to, thirdly diversification of the sources of our tourism, the variety of countries from which our tourists come. The maximum of diversification, the minimum of reliance upon one country or a handful of countries means the greater your independence, the less able certain people are to squeeze you, pressurize you and blackmail you.[30]

And Grenada has certainly been able to make progress here, particularly in the banana trade, whereby now a banana agreement exists between Grenada and the German Democratic Republic. Britain has become the major importer of egg plants, one of Grenada's newest export crops, and the Soviet Union has agreed to buy a regular supply of nutmegs for the next five years, thus saving for Grenada the thousands and thousands of dollars that used to be lost every year upon Dutch brokerage.

However, despite these successes, the Grenadian experience clearly shows how imperialism manipulates the multinationals to create industrial havoc and destabilization. This was illustrated with particular vividness when the Manager of the Grenada Electricity Company (the majority of whose shares were owned by the British multinational, the Commonwealth Development Corporation) was implicated, alongside the leadership of the Public Workers' Union, in the disruptions of March 1981. The Manager, Rodney George, had openly declared at a Public Workers' Union meeting that he would 'put the country into darkness' if the People's Revolutionary Government did not bend to the 70 per cent pay demand, and there was a clear victimization of state-owned institutions which were getting more than their fair share of blackouts — particularly government hotels that were filled with guests who had arrived for the Second Anniversary celebrations. The ghosts of Chile-style destabilization were being roused from limbo.

While George was sparking his rhetoric at Public Workers' Union meetings, (even though he was not a member and did not work in a state institution), his own workers at GRENLEC had a different message about working conditions there. Dudley Pierre of Boca, who had been working for the company for more than ten years had this to say:

> The company always says that the generators are to be serviced after three years or so. They, however, do not carry out these instructions, making it harder for the workers and everyone combined when they break down. When all the machines are of a poor quality, one breaks down and there is no spare one working. So there will be blackouts. In addition, maintenance men are forced to work so hurriedly that the best cannot be done.
>
> Most workers here work very hard, and seeing that this work is with electricity and many heavy machines, some sort of meaningful pension scheme ought to be available to us.

Another worker was quoted in *The Free West Indian* as saying:

> They don't put any money in for research and improvements. They promise training when you take the job, but when you arrive here you see it's different.
>
> If you look at CDC's policy in Africa and India they spend a lot of money there. This is because they also get the benefits down there, the mineral wealth and so on. It's all a part of their imperialist aims. In Grenada, however, you see a vast difference. They feel they have bled us dry and that this day is coming to an end.'[31]

He couldn't have been more right and, in May 1981, that day came. The CDC, Esso and Barclays Bank combined further to disrupt Grenada's electricity supply. First of all the CDC pleaded that it had no money to buy the necessary fuel to continue production — although it was simultaneously shipping home to England its normal quota of profits and dividends and refusing to re-invest in the Grenada plant, even though the machines were now little more than museum pieces. Then Barclays refused to grant a loan and, finally, Esso obligingly threatened to stop the supply of fuel unless immediate bills were settled. There was real counter-revolutionary harmony in the midst of this apparent chaos, and the situation was only resolved when the People's Revolutionary Government stepped in and acquired majority shares in the electricity company.

Destabilization through the Local Bourgeoisie: The Grenadian Voice

If the GRENLEC crisis was a blatant example of the power of international industrial destabilization, reactionary sections of the local national bourgeoisie were also frantically playing their part. These elements made up the 'Committee of 26', who published in St George's a CIA-backed journal, *The Grenadian Voice,* in May 1981. In his Heroes' Day speech, Bishop characterized them in this way:

> A second category, comrades, you can broadly regard as being the unpatriotic, reactionary, the power-seeking national bourgeoisie in our country. In other words the biggest man, the biggest exploiters, the biggest parasites, the biggest vampires, the biggest bloodsuckers in the country. That is another category that the CIA and imperialism look for because they recognize that some of the elements of that class fear that they have lost their political power; that they are losing their political hold over the masses and they are afraid that their economic base which they have built by the exploitation and suffering of our people, they are afraid too that that is disappearing.
>
> It is no accident then, bearing this in mind, that so many of the elements of the 'Committee of 26' come from the biggest and most unpatriotic landowners in the country, those who are opposed to land reform, those who are opposed to workers' participation; those who are opposed to the Trade Union Movement — and Comrade Coard sends them the annual income tax statement and they get a big accountant to fill up a form, to keep two books for them, to pretend they make no profit, they getting fatter and fatter and fatter and you see more houses go up, you see more land acquired and you see more and more cars and luxury items — but they never make profits!
>
> These same elements that oppose every benefit that the poor in our country receive, who are opposed to free health care because they can always send their wife on a plane to Trinidad or Barbados; those who oppose free secondary education because it mean that the little black men son will have to go to school and rub shoulders

with their nice sons and daughters and transfer some kind of brain disease to them. These elements who oppose the reducing of rent on the backs of our people because they own the buildings and they charge the rent; those who oppose free milk distribution in our country because if there is free milk then the Dano and the Nestlé's and the Nesquick and all the other brands of milk that they bring in will not be able to be sold anymore. So they oppose the free milk too. Those who are afraid of the benefits the masses are now getting because they recognize — quite correctly — that what they are facing in this land is a People's Revolution, a revolution for the poor and working masses of our country.

The Grenadian Voice issue was a classic example of CIA manipulation of local reaction. When he exposed the entire intrigue in the same speech, the Prime Minister was clear in pointing out what a miniscule section of the overall population compose such elements:

> In a fighting population of 110,000 people, you are talking of less than a few hundred people total that imperialism can hope to reach and to induce and seduce. We have to recognize, comrades, that that is not a big lot, that it is not a lot we are looking for. It is a tiny minority that choose to go the way of counter-revolution. But they must understand the price of counter-revolution, they must understand that.

The first news that the People's Revolutionary Government had of the existence of what turned out to be an intricate CIA plot, came through the blunder of a US State Department official in Barbados. The official, his tongue slipping, inadvertently revealed to Kenrick Radix, the Minister of Justice and Industrial Development, that Grenada was shortly to see the publication of a new newspaper. As it later came to light, this newspaper was just the first step in an intrigue of various stages:

> Stage one was the newspaper. Stage two, as they analyze it, is when the paper close down, because they know that we would not allow a counter-revolutionary newspaper. Then Stage three in the plan was that after the paper was closed down, they use regional and international propaganda against the country and pretend it is about freedom of the press. Then they were going to try to get a strike going in our country and we know for a fact that even today, one of them was trying to incite dockworkers to take strike action, even today as I am speaking to you.

We know that the fifth stage that they have is to try and squeeze the economy. We know that this can take many forms and we are going to be looking for every single one of them.

We have to understand that this plan we are seeing now, the first element of which is the newspaper, is a different plan to all that went before, because this is not the type of plan in which local counters, local opportunists are being used. This is not the kind of plan where the ganja capitalists who are in the employment of the CIA are being used. To understand this plan fully you have to do a piece of magic in your heads, you have to forget the names of those twenty-six and instead of those twenty-six names you write one single word — you write CIA!

The identities of the twenty-six were largely predictable: owners and shareholders of large local enterprises and rural estates were well represented, plus a trade union leader and Alister Hughes — the local correspondent of the Caribbean News Agency (CANA) and occasional contributor to *The Times* of London. Many of these elements were ex-members of the Grenada National Party (GNP), the ineffectual and conciliating opposition to Gairy for over twenty years, and defenders of the interest of the plantocrats and the local commercial class. The trade union leader was the same man who had been made a Senator after his sell-out of the dockworkers in 1974, and the others had similar records of self-interest and betrayal.

Their plan, however, far from appealing to the mass of the people, only incurred their wrath. There were large demonstrations outside their houses, and this unpredicted reaction caused a swift exit from the country for some of them, who thirty-six hours after the publication of the paper were nowhere to be found or be seen. Others hastily tried to cover themselves by saying that their names appeared in the paper without their consent or their knowledge. It was yet another demonstration to the people of the duplicity of these particular standard-bearers of the local bourgeoisie, posing as patriots, yet seeking to turn back everything that the mass of the people had won for themselves, and the Government's decision to close down the paper because of its direct link with the CIA was greeted with general approval and enthusiasm. The commercial class in particular had been knocked even further back in their destabilization potential.

They had previously lost their importing monopolies in

certain staple foods like sugar and rice — which early on in the
Revolution the Government had very wisely passed to the
Marketing and National Importing Board, a state enterprise
which now handled all imports of these vital commodities. This,
at one blow, prevented the speculation, manufactured shortages, hoarding and panic buying which had been used as lethal
destabilizing weapons against other revolutionary governments. Now, after the failure and defeat of *The Grenadian
Voice*, any credibility they had left disappeared entirely as the
people brought their conscious minds to bear on the episode. As
Grenadians indignantly asserted that *The Grenadian Voice* was
not their voice, *The Free West Indian* was there to listen and
report:

As far as I see, these people can't communicate with me, they are not
our type. They never speak to people. They never had a meeting
where they told people what they're really about. This paper, as far
as I can see, is really their voice, and they're calling it ours.

Again, the kind of people, like Toppin and them, they give
people too much pressure already for anyone to listen to them. I see
them as men who just want to split up the progress of the country.
The PRG is progressive and them kind of people don't want
progress in this time. I support the PRG's move to deal with the
situation.

Ian Samuel, La Mode

I feel that this paper is only the voice of a few people, and anybody
who have sense could see that. I see the PRG's action as a good
move, because these kind of things could be dangerous for the
Revolution.

Mighty Skef, Beaulieu

Government should write a letter to Toppin telling him to treat his
workers better.

Mrs Mills, St. George's

These people are business people and they should not have called
their newspaper *The Grenadian Voice*. They do not represent the
majority of Grenadians as they try to make out. I really support the
PRG action, because everyone should see that the PRG stands fully
behind the poor people of the country.

Carmen St. Clair, St Andrew's

Where I-man and the brethren on the blocks got the paper, we burn it man. I-man don't support them kind of political issue; it is just another power struggle. Those men are not interested in the masses, they can't speak for I.

Lumumba Ababa, Sauteurs

Those men were out of place and rude to publish a paper stating they are the 'Grenadian Voice', whereas the Government and the people are the Grenadian voices. It is a good move by the PRG to close it down, but I feel they should be put under heavier manners.

Adrian Church, Mt. Gay

The overall aim of the paper was to overthrow the Government. The plan was to start off in a small way, which seemed harmless, and to gradually go on to have political implications. What they would have finally done was to destabilize the Revolution. When you check the names of the men who published the paper, it is the same old bourgeois clique who are not interested in the masses making progress. The PRG made the appropriate move to close it down.

Byron Benjamin, St. Paul's[32]

Diplomatic Destabilization

The diplomatic struggle is another dimension of the overall struggle between the progressive forces worldwide, and the destabilizing campaigns of imperialism. At the same time that the US has constantly been offering inducements for other Caribbean states to cut their economic ties with Grenada, much diplomatic pressure for the international isolation of Grenada has also been applied. Grenadian ministers and diplomats have been shunned on visits to the US and have been refused the customary protocol and security measures. Dessima Williams, Grenada's Ambassador to the Organization of American States (OAS) has not been formally recognized by the US Government, and Grenadian ministers and government personnel passing through Barbados — acting as the willing US proxy in the Eastern Caribbean — have been brutally and insultingly treated. Unison Whiteman, who was Minister of Agriculture at the time, was manhandled and physically searched, his diplomatic privileges scorned and his baggage cut open in defiance of his diplomatic passport, when he passed through Grantley

Adams International Airport in Barbados in November 1980. The objective clearly is to attempt to internationally humiliate the Grenada Revolution and demonstrate disrespect and contempt for its representatives.

The harassment at the same airport of Grenadian citizens and visitors to Grenada has sporadically continued — intensifying particularly during times of national events and festivals such as the 13 March celebrations. A common strategy is to force passengers to stay overnight or an extra day or two in Barbados because of 'problems' with bookings. The Mighty Guava had this to say in his calypso 'Please Don't Let Them Stop Us', which made the finals of the 1981 Carnival Calypso Competition and exhorted Grenadians to work determinedly on to see their own International Airport Project completed, so as to end all the harassment in Barbados, the 'lost' luggage and the other inconveniences:

> We have seen our luggage lost
> And we know what it cost,
> That is why things have to stop,
> Our country must go to the top –
> No overnighting in Barbados
> Because this airport will bring
> More tourists to our shores.

Another grotesque example of the harassment of a Grenadian citizen abroad — this time on US-controlled territory — was in May 1982 when Suzanne Berkeley, a young Grenadian delegate from the Catholic Youth Council, was detained, bullied and threatened by the US Immigration Service at Puerto Rico's main airport when she entered that colony with a valid visa to attend a religious conference. She was locked up in a toilet and interrogated with such questions as 'Do you believe in socialism?' After a harrowing experience, Berkeley was released only to be deported, despite international protests and appeals from the conference organizers. It was enough, clearly, that she was from Grenada.[33] Such was the value of President Reagan's words in reply to Prime Minister Bishop's congratulatory telegram on the former's election to the American Presidency: '. . . looking forward to a mutual effort to promote friendly relations between our two nations.'

For the present US Administration has made determined efforts to force Grenada into isolation amongst her Caribbean neighbours. Its most clumsy effort in this direction was in July 1981, when a Southern congressman with a blatantly racist record, one Bill Nelson, visited the region and while in St Lucia called upon regional governments to terminate their relations with Grenada! Coming from such quarters, this buffoonery could hardly have been treated seriously, despite the amount of Caribbean media treatment it received. However, dollars speak louder and, in June 1981, two regional governments were offered money for a particular project if they publicly condemned the Grenada Government. Prime Minister Tom Adams of Barbados and Prime Minister Eugenia Charles of Dominica have several times launched verbal attacks on Grenada, but apart from a little US bribe money these have earned them little throughout the region other than apt nicknames: 'Yard Fowl' and 'Mother Hen'.

The US strategy of diplomatic isolation for Grenada is being applied simultaneously with the build-up of a much more forceful US military presence in the Eastern Caribbean. Since November 1979 there has been a Caribbean Task Force based in Miami, and this contains a rapid deployment force capable of direct response to any progressive or revolutionary development in the region, along with a significant increase in military aid to all Eastern Caribbean states, excluding Grenada. In this context, although the US has not accredited its Eastern Caribbean Ambassador to Grenada, as it did up to 1981, it has increased its diplomatic — and hence its CIA — personnel in the region.

The US diplomatic freeze grew even more icy in February 1981, when Sally Shelton, the outgoing US Ambassador to the Eastern Caribbean, decided to forego a farewell protocol visit to Grenada, something which is conventional diplomatic politeness. In an open snub, she claimed that Grenada had rebuffed US attempts to improve relations and that there was a lack of interest on *Grenada*'s part to add any meaning to relations between the two countries. For her part, Grenada made several subsequent diplomatic efforts, by letters sent by Prime Minister Bishop directly to President Reagan, to create communication between the two governments, but only the most summary and unhelpful replies were ever received. Again, after the remarks by Shelton, the Grenadian masses had the last word in *The Free West Indian*:

I see Shelton as defending her own personal interest in trying to isolate Grenada. This Revolution is a popular one, even though we have problems. Elections is really not a concern of Sally Shelton or any non-Grenadians. It is obvious that the US does not want to develop relations with Grenada. Recently when the PRG asked the US to accept our Dessima Williams as Ambassador, they refused.

Albert Benjamin, River Road

I feel that Shelton does not understand that Grenadian people make their own decisions. In fact she does not even understand the basic laws of protocol. She behaves as if the US is some type of breadwinner for Grenada. They offered only 5,000 dollars to us after the Revo when they spend thousands more every year on arms. All her human rights brango talk are really lies in the attempt to isolate Grenada — but I feel that Grenadians must try to learn more about international affairs, to understand more about the international situation.

Lewis Henry, Victoria

By December 1982 the US Vice-President, George Bush, at a Miami-based conference on the Caribbean and Latin America, was declaring that Grenada was economically weak and dependent. The PRG pointed out in its reply that in August 1982 the World Bank Report on Grenada had in fact attested to the nation's striking economic progress! The report admitted to Grenada's positive economic growth averaging 3 per cent per annum, while the US economy was moving in reverse.

The British Conservative Government of Margaret Thatcher was giving her usual slavish demonstration of carrying the US train in relation to Grenada — though the previous Labour Government had hardly been very encouraging either when it refused to grant export licences for the sale of two armoured cars to the People's Revolutionary Government. The Tories, once in power, made their attitude clear in a bizarre statement from Nicholas Ridley, their man in the Foreign Office: 'Grenada is in the process of establishing a kind of society of which the British Government disapproves, irrespective of whether the people of Grenada want it or not.' This piece of diplomatic riches was matched by the statement of another Foreign Office man, Richard Luce, who on a tour of the Eastern Caribbean in early 1982, while the entire population of Grenada were engaged in mass consultations to formulate the national budget in an unique and unprecedented process of mass democracy and participation, peevishly complained that he would not extend his visit to Grenada as there was no democracy there!

Economic Destabilization

The pattern of US economic destabilization against the People's Revolutionary Government was established very quickly after the 13 March Revolution, when Grenada raised the possibility of economic aid with Frank Ortiz, who was then the US Ambassador to the Eastern Caribbean. The latter's response was to offer a paltry five thousand dollars from the embassy's discretionary fund, and that was the limit of generosity from the richest country in the world to one of the smallest! And this bounty was offered alongside a warning that the US would view with displeasure any close links developing between Grenada and Cuba. At the same time the CIA organized the planting of a 'travel scare' against Grenada through travel agencies in North America. An unofficial survey done in Washington shortly after that time revealed that nineteen out of twenty-five travel agencies contacted were openly discouraging their customers from visiting Grenada.

The following January, after severe rainstorms, the Grenadian Government asked the US again for bilateral assistance to help rebuild roads, bridges and schools that had been badly damaged or destroyed. This request was completely ignored. When Grenada then turned to the Organization of American States' Emergency Unit, FONDEM, for relief assistance, the USAID delegate openly raised doubts whether Grenada needed such support and insisted that an investigation be made into the application, a tactic which delayed the much-needed assistance.

During the same year the US Government moved again to block assistance, this time to the hurricane-blasted Grenadian banana farmers, even though aid was given to the other three members of the Windward Islands Banana Association (WIN-BAN) — St Lucia, Dominica and St Vincent. This was clearly a direct economic snub to the People's Revolutionary Government and yet another attempt to divide Grenada from the institutions of the Eastern Caribbean.

During April 1981, the European Economic Community hosted a co-financing conference in Brussels in a bid to raise the thirty million US dollars needed for the completion of Grenada's New International Airport Project. The US State

Department constantly tried to undermine the organization and execution of this event, attempting to dissuade EEC member countries from attending and lying about the airport's new function by declaring it to be a potential Cuban base for intervention in Africa and disruption of US shipping lanes. But, as the *Caribbean Contact* of December 1981 commented: '. . . the tiny Caribbean island of 110,000 countered with some skilful diplomacy of its own, and in the end emerged triumphant with a cheque for six million Eastern Caribbean dollars from the EEC. The victory for Grenada was all the more remarkable because the EEC provided the money as a grant, rather than a loan.'

But this particular effort at international economic sabotage was only the most publicized example of many such US initiatives. Time after time attempts have been made to persuade international economic agencies against funding technically viable and positive projects for the development of Grenada. The World Bank has been consistently lobbied by the US and was persuaded not to endorse Grenada's public investment programme. There was also direct interference by the US member on the Board of Directors of the International Monetary Fund (IMF) in 1981, when Grenada applied for a loan of 8.17 million US dollars under its extended loan facility, to finance various projects in agriculture, agro-industry, tourism and housing.

The continued efforts to isolate Grenada politically from other Caribbean nations were escalated again in June 1981, when the US offered the Caribbean Development Bank a four million dollar loan for 'basic human needs' in the region, on the condition that Grenada be excluded. Despite the political and ideological differences in the region, all the English-speaking Caribbean nations closed ranks and refused an offer made in such divisive terms. Thus, as Bishop pointed out during his speech at the opening of the Socialist International Conference held in Grenada in July 1981, they had struck an important blow for Caribbean unity: 'Our friends in the region, different countries in CARICOM, stood up to this latest blatant attempt on the part of the US Administration to divide and rule the region and to attempt to subvert this Caribbean regional institution.'

Throughout 1982, destabilization emerged in its latest and perhaps most dangerous form, as an 'Aid Plan'. The talk and preparations from the Reagan Administration concerning a 'Mini-Marshall Plan' for the entire region was directed specifically at the US client states, vindicating the Puerto Rican 'Free Enterprise' model. It was rooted in the notion of arresting any further genuine economic independence in the Caribbean Basin, particularly in the shape of countries pursuing revolutionary transformations in their economies like Cuba, Nicaragua and Grenada. The US idea of channelling 'billions of dollars' to shore up free enterprise in the Caribbean is transparently the old 'Monroe Doctrine' in a new form: to sow disunity and division within the region and sabotage genuine economic development or any form of popular government which threatens US hegemony in its 'backyard'.

All this economic destabilization was occurring at a critical time for the Grenadian economy. The years 1979–81 included serious hurricane damage in August 1979 and early 1980, accompanied by heavy flooding: 27 per cent of the country's nutmeg crop, 40 per cent of the banana crop and 19 per cent of all cocoa production was totally destroyed, with an estimated damage of twenty million US dollars. This was followed by a further blast of torrential rains in April 1981, when a further five million US dollars damage was done. In addition, world market prices of Grenada's principal commodity exports fell by 22 per cent in 1980. Cocoa prices fell from £2,000 per tonne to £1,100 in the period 1979–80, resulting in a 3.4 million US dollars reduction in earnings from these exports. Nutmegs and bananas told a similar story, nutmegs being hit particularly seriously with a glut on the world market, leaving Grenada holding almost a year's production unsold, which represented a loss of some thirty five million Eastern Caribbean dollars. And these problems were compounded by an 8.8 per cent reduction in stay-over visitors, thus hitting the tourist industry. This was due not only to the world recession, but also in no small part to the active campaign of propaganda destabilization orchestrated by the US Government.

By early 1982 the 'Mini-Marshall Plan' had developed into the high-sounding Caribbean Basin Initiative (CBI), but by then the original conception of a non-political discriminatory and non-military aid plan for the entire region, with other donor countries like Canada, Mexico, France, West Germany and Venezuela contributing their ideas and inputs, had degenerated into a US support package to back up what Washington called 'friendly, democratic governments' like Duarte in El Salvador, the Military Junta in Guatemala, Duvalier in Haiti and the increasingly backward Seaga régime in Jamaica. It was married to a military component to provide 'security' assistance to the US proxy governments in the region. In addition, the actual sum in question was not the vision of 'billions of dollars' but a far more modest 350 million dollars which, as Bishop clarified during his analysis of the CBI (which he called 'the con-game of the century'), was only equivalent to the profits made by a large US company over the space of three days! 'How shameful it is to reflect,' he continued, 'that the present military manoeuvres, announced at the same time as the CBI, cost more than the entire CBI plan.'[34]

Later in the month, Unison Whiteman, the Minister of Foreign Affairs, speaking to a CARICOM conference of Foreign Ministers, called upon the other Caribbean nations to reject the plan, pointing out that the vast majority of the CBI money was heading directly to support the military dictatorship in El Salvador, and that in fact just ten million US dollars was intended for the Eastern Caribbean. This was, said Whiteman, like feeding an ox with a pea! He explained how the plan sought to divide and split the CARICOM nations, by by-passing Caribbean institutions set up specifically to receive aid, like the Caribbean Development Bank, and refusing to deal with the region as a single economic unit — which was the very purpose of CARICOM. Thus the CBI struck at the very heart of the progressive aspirations of Caribbean unity.[35]

As a direct result of Grenada's regional campaign exposing Reaganomics, other Caribbean governments were soon revising and changing their attitudes to the CBI plan and beginning to see through its cosmetics. This new Caribbean scepticism about Reagan's intentions was made more profound by the latter's disastrous visit to Barbados during mid-1982 on a 'working holiday', when his security aides pushed aside Barbadian pressmen with racist insults and where the President isolated himself from anything home-produced in the Caribbean even to the extent of bringing with him his own drinking water and toilet tissue. His Caribbean flirtation was later befuddled even further by his own Senate Foreign Relations Committee's outright rejection of the CBI, and at the time of writing the celluloid cowboy's schemes for the Caribbean are far from being implemented.

As Finance Minister Bernard Coard commented in an interview in June, 1982:

> The 'CBI' is an attempt to maintain the structures of domination, exploitation and oppression by totally inadequate bribery. It will not even meet the challenge from a purely opportunistic bribery point of view, nor would it, even if the bribe were large enough, succeed in quenching the thirst of the Caribbean people for genuine democracy in matters both political and economic. Reagan's 'CBI' has no chance of succeeding in its imperialist objectives.[36]

Propaganda Destabilization

> When they speak of a free press they speak of when the same man or the same group of men or companies who run all the newspapers, run all the radio stations, run all the television stations – you are talking about the same people pretending and using different voices.
>
> *Maurice Bishop:*
> Heroes' Day Speech, 16 June 1981

Nothing has done more to expose the way the Caribbean regional press is intimately linked to wider US imperialist interest, than the organized and co-ordinated campaign of lies and slander it has waged against the Grenada Revolution. The examples of propaganda destabilization in Guyana under Cheddi Jagan's People's Progressive Party, the media blitz suffered by Allende's Popular Unity Government in Chile and spearheaded by the national daily *El Mercurio,* and the outright war declared upon the Manley Government in Jamaica by *The Daily Gleaner*, were cogent examples to the People's Revolutionary Government of how the imperialist press and its local branches would work against them too. Some of the hugest and richest media interests in the world have attacked Grenada, with its tiny land mass and its population equivalent to a small English provincial city. *The Boston Globe. The Washington Post, The New York Times, The Wall Street Journal, The Miami Herald, The Los Angeles Times, Newsweek* with its headline 'Tiny Exporter of Revolution' and *Time* with its article 'The Reluctant Revolution' have all clamoured to join the act. *Bunte* magazine of West Germany claimed that Grenada had a Soviet missile base on its central hills with warheads aimed at neigh-

bouring islands, *The Times* and the hand of Alister Hughes
claimed that there were no human rights in Grenada, and a BBC
television documentary consolidated these lies by asserting that
political detainees were being brutally tortured and that *three*
airstrips were being built at Point Salines so that again Grenada
could mastermind attacks on all its neighbours. In his speech at
the opening of the Conference of Caribbean Journalists, Bishop
dealt with these stories, and extracts from this speech are
reproduced as an appendix to this book.

The fact that the People's Revolutionary Government has
consistently exposed the monopolistic ownership and unde-
mocratic procedures of the Caribbean press magnates, has
clearly infuriated them. As Bishop pointed out: 'several of these
newspapers in the region are owned by the same big businessmen and corporations with a vested interest to maintain the
cruel, unjust, exploitative and profiteering system we live
under.' For example, Ken Gordon, who owns the *Trinidad
Express*, also shares in the Barbados *Nation* and is involved in
the Barbados *Sun*. He is also in the Inter-American Press
Association and the Caribbean Publishers' and Broadcasters'
Association and linked with the Caribbean Press Council. The
Trinidad Express also owned a massive 4,062 shares in *The
Torchlight*, which after appearing to be initially welcoming to
the Grenada Revolution, gradually began to introduce into its
columns more and more insinuations and outright lies about the
process, and to reprint hostile editorials from its parent the
Trinidad Express. For example, in the issue of 5 August 1979 it
republished the assertion that 'we can conceivably wake up one
morning to find a Cuban base located smack bang in the middle
of the Eastern Caribbean'. Simultaneously, the St George's-
based paper openly published the names and photographs
identifying the Prime Minister's security men and gave to the
world the exact locations of Grenada's defence installations.

The Torchlight soon became a continuous source of destabilization and ally of almost every force that was trying to turn
back the Revolution. It promoted an anti-communist editorial
position, attacking the Cuban technical assistance and casting
aspersions on Cuban internationalists like the medical teams
who were making life so much better for the working people of
Grenada. If the stories had been written by Grenadians from
Grenada, their credibility might have been greater, but *The
Torchlight* fast became a hotch-potch of unsubstantiated

rumour, sheer speculation and a digest of imported, replicated anti-government scandal with reprints of reactionary cartoons from *The Gleaner*, including one showing Fidel Castro 'fishing' to catch Grenada. The paper began to spread rumours about food shortages, about Radio Free Grenada 'minimizing' and seeking to axe religious programmes — 'Christians stand firm!' they proclaimed in headlines — and these rumours were clearly organized to dovetail with other absurdities circulating at the time about the PRG introducing ration cards and confiscating furniture and other personal effects. Simultaneously, articles were reprinted by an American 'photo-journalist', Fred Ward, whose previous work had appeared in the *National Geographic Magazine*, about 'Life in Cuba', including the predictable anti-Castro assertions and quoting one particular interviewee as saying, 'it was a lot better when the Americans were here'. In the very same issue there was a striking headline, quoting one John Harrell, the 'Founder of the Christian Conservative Churches', and declaring that 'Communism is the boiled-down evil of all the generations.'

Later that same year, the People's Revolutionary Government, well instructed by previous events in Chile and Jamaica, closed down the newspaper. This was immediately interpreted by the press monopolists in the Caribbean as a heinous blow against the 'freedom of the press', and the Government's gutty response to such open harassment was viewed as the worst crime of all — an attack upon Mr Gordon's shares. Certainly since then the bile emitting from the *Trinidad Express* towards Grenada has been so bitter as to make its pronouncements even more unbelievable. But ironically, the continuation of *The Torchlight* story was really a new beginning for its workers, all members of the Technical and Allied Workers' Union, who in August 1981, after the management of the company had abandoned them owing them substantial arrears of salary, took over *The Torchlight* company, Grenada Publishers Limited, and set up their own co-operative. The testimonies of the workers exposed that the bastion of the 'free press' in Grenada had exploited them with low wages, bad working conditions and imperious management for over a quarter of a century.[37]

The story of *Time* magazine's visit to Grenada, and the professional antics of its correspondent, Bill McWhirter, were skilfully monitored and later told in *The Free West Indian* by St. Lucian journalist Earl Bousquet:

THE LIE OF THE TIME

Looking at the list of foreign journalists here for the Second Festival of the Revolution, my attention was attracted by the name William McWhirter. I recalled it from several articles he had written in the USA's *Time* magazine about Cuba and Nicaragua. McWhirter is *Time*'s Caribbean Bureau chief, and his presence made me uneasy. Those pieces I had read were subtle, sarcastic attacks on the revolutionary processes in Cuba and Nicaragua, and I felt his story on Grenada would be no different.

I decided to observe him from time to time, to see how he went about covering the most important event in Grenada. As soon as he arrived, he demanded that the staff at the media centre arrange an interview for him with Prime Minister Maurice Bishop. And he called them up several times, complaining about their taking too long to arrange it. Within hours, he had contacted several other persons for the same purpose.

I soon met and spoke to him. His behaviour was that of the typical bourgeois journalist who saw himself as more intelligent than everyone else. But it was on 13 March that I really came face to face with McWhirter's arrogance. He had gone to Queen's Park to cover the rally, but took no notes except the names of the speakers. He had a tape recorder but wasn't using it. When Prime Minister Bishop started speaking, he started taping. But when the Prime Minister started exposing the US Administration's cutbacks on programmes which benefited poor Americans. McWhirter switched off his tape, left the press area and disappeared into the crowd. He was not seen again at the rally.

I told a colleague that I thought McWhirter had written his story about the rally before it started. Given their political position, I knew it was something such American reporters did when their overall objective on a particular event has been clear in their minds long before they arrive on the scene: they write their story first, and make the necessary amendments later.

Only a few hours after the rally I had my second major observation of McWhirter's arrogance towards progressive Caribbean people. It was at the reception at the Prime Minister's Office on the night of 13 March. On the day he arrived McWhirter had met Renwick Rose, General Secretary of the opposition United People Movement (UPM) of St Vincent, an invited guest to the festival who happened to be staying at the same hotel. McWhirter had tried several times to get Rose's views on the Grenada Revolution, but fearing he would be misquoted, Rose refrained from answering. At the party McWhirter confronted Rose once again, this time tugging at the latter's shoulders. Obviously annoyed, Rose told him that all he wanted to say was that he wanted the United States to keep its hands off Grenada. Dissatisfied, McWhirter stared at Rose and called him an 'island fool'.

But I did not have to wait long for someone to put McWhirter in his place. The following morning he turned up at the Prime Minister's press conference for foreign journalists. I felt sure he would try to jam the Prime Minister with some off-beat questions. It soon happened. Prime Minister Bishop was answering another journalist's question on foreign policy when McWhirter suddenly cut into the Prime Minister's reply with a question: 'You say that Grenada is nonaligned. Then why is it that you always vote with the Soviet Union and Cuba on every issue at the United Nations?'

The Prime Minister said he was unaware of this. Grenada did not turn around to see how other countries were voting before she voted.

McWhirter cut him short with another question: 'Then tell us at least one occasion that you did not vote the same way as the Soviets and the Cubans?'

The Prime Minister repeated that he did not monitor how other countries voted. Grenada did not necessarily see nonalignment as neutrality, he said, and had a firm position on most issues. Grenada was pleased when other countries shared its positions. If a vote were to be taken at the UN the following day on El Salvador for example, he said Grenada knew how she would vote, and if it had to look around to see who was voting with her, the country she would really like to see 'is the United States'.

That certainly put McWhirter in his place, the other journalists present burst into laughter and applause.

Two weeks later, on 30 March, McWhirter's report entitled 'The Reluctant Revolution', appeared. No one was surprised by his not-too-subtle effort to imply the close relations between Grenada and revolutionary Cuba. Once again I had come face to face with another bold-faced and blatant attempt to misinform the world's peoples about the Grenada Revolution. Considering the millions of people around the world who read *Time* magazine, a significant amount will be misled, and deliberately so, because the writer knew all along that his report was inaccurate and unfair.

The report lacked sources, and in typical *Time* style, it quoted unidentified persons and, in one case, a known opponent to the

Revolution. While conceding that the Revolution had brought benefits and had improved considerably the material being of the people, McWhirter nonetheless gave a grim picture of Grenada as a country where people have turned their backs on the Revolution. To back up this lie, the man who disappeared from the park at the beginning of the Prime Minister's address said that, 'of the 6,000 people present, a full third left before the Prime Minister stepped on the podium, and most of the rest did not even bother to applaud' when he finished speaking.

When I remember the prolonged applause that followed the Prime Minister's speech, I took a photocopy of McWhirter's report and filed it away, among so many others I have, as yet more evidence of the US monopoly press efforts at propaganda destabilization against the Grenada Revolution. And I wondered how many times McWhirter had prostituted his skills for the benefit of corporate America and imperialism.[38]

Bousquet's careful observations illustrated absolutely the role of this 'free press' in relation to the Grenada Revolution, and the Prime Minister underlined what *Time*'s Caribbean cousins were moving towards:

When they speak of a 'free press' comrades, we are to understand that they talk of rights to have journalistic licences, they have the right to publish freely what they like. But this journalistic licence simply means the right to print lies and slander people, the right to incite people to violence, the right to hold one position only and to pretend that that position represents the whole truth. That is what they mean by journalistic licence. When they speak of 'independence' we have to ask what independence and independence for whom? We have to recognize that it is the same voice with one idea that the voice of the people, the voice of the poor working masses can never get expression in their journal or in their publications.

Think of *The Torchlight* and the role *The Torchlight* played. It was always a good thing, always good news, it was always a free press to expose military camps when they were established, it was always a good thing! It was always excellent news to reprint garbage and rubbish from abroad like the article appearing in the West German magazine — the article that said we had underground submarines in Grenada. That kind of article is in accordance with the freedom of the press. But when the masses are meeting, when the masses are engaged in productive activity — that does not require a free press, that then becomes unimportant news for the class and the interest they represent.

We must never forget the role of *The Torchlight* with the rastafarian brethren in our country, a newspaper that over the years consistently attacked the rastas, called them all kinds of names — and attacked Comrade Radix and myself whenever we went to court as lawyers to defend these brethren. Then remember what we saw in September 1979 when *The Torchlight* opportunistically pretended to be a champion of the rastas, to go around talking how the rastas were being terrorized and brutalized by the People's Revolutionary Government, how they were being killed in the hills and how the time has come for the rastas to take a response against Babylon. If you could imagine *The Torchlight* with that level of deceitfulness and hypocrisy and taking that kind of position and playing that kind of role.

The media of film and television have also played an overt destabilizing role against Grenada. In January 1981 the American Security Council Foundation and the Coalition for Peace through Strength released a 25-minute, 16 mm colour film entitled *Attack on the Americas*, which systematically denounced the Cuban, Nicaraguan and Grenadian revolutions. Millions of dollars were spent on distributing this film among television stations, public schools and civic groups in the USA. This assault has been increased by the CBS–TV five-part series screened in New York called *The Prisoner and the Police State*. No evidence was presented to support the accusations of a denial of human rights in Grenada and the rise of a totalitarian state under the People's Revolutionary Government. The CBS then followed this up with a 'Special Report' on Grenada, highlighting the statement made by the local Roman Catholic bishop, Bishop Sydney Charles, that the benefits brought by the Revolution had come at too high a price, alluding to the fraternal bond between the people of Grenada and Cuba. It was a provocative move to stir up the Church against the PRG and preceded another attempt in the same direction in July 1982, when Alister Hughes, speaking at the annual convention of Eugenia Charles' Dominica Freedom Party, called upon the Church as the true life's blood of democracy, openly to resist the Revolution.

Every conceivable monopolist US media agency has set its target as Grenada. Not only regional and international press agencies like CANA, Associated Press, Reuters, United Press and Agence France — but also the hostile radio stations such as Radio Antilles, Radio Bonaire, Radio 610 and the newly established Voice of America, station in Antigua, with its powerful uni-directional southern signal. Radio Antilles, for example, on 8 December 1981, aired an item concerning a Trinidadian lawyer named Ramesh Maharaj and his 'Trinidad and Tobago Human Rights Bureau'. He claimed that he had unearthed evidence to show that two detainees in prison awaiting trial in connexion with the 19 June bombing, had broken fingers and toes, and scars where their skin had been peeled off with pliers. This fabrication of horrors was exposed as Maharaj's macabre fantasy when medical reports, made in the same week as the allegations and saying that the prisoners were in excellent health with no sign of any external or internal injuries, were presented to the *Trinidad Express* and the *Guardian*, who had, of course, picked up the story from Radio Antilles with relish, but never sought to include a disclaimer with quite the same keenness. Added to all this, Cyrus and Herry saw their own opportunity to create even more propaganda destabilization by publishing a journal, *The Grenadian*, full of muck-raking rumours against the private lives of members of the People's Revolutionary Government, purporting to give the 'real facts' behind the Revolution and calling for its overthrow. Since publication, thousands of free copies have been distributed throughout the Caribbean, and also in New York, London, Toronto and Washington, proving that the enterprise is very generously funded indeed.

The international campaign of lies against Grenada reached its most sinister level in May 1981, when the United States International Communications Agency (USICA), the propaganda arm of the US State Department, summoned the editors of all the major Caribbean newspapers to a special conference in Washington. A featured, if unlisted, agenda item was 'How to deal with Grenada'. In his speech to the journalists Bishop speaks of the shameless results of these deliberations and the identical front-page anti-Grenada editorials that followed in five Caribbean newspapers. Here indeed once more was the boasted 'independence' of the free press and the full expression of journalistic licence.

As the Prime Minister called for an intensification of the struggle to achieve the New International Information Order at the Trade Union Conference for the Unity and Solidarity of

Caribbean Workers in Grenada in November 1981, the delegates *and* the Grenadian masses present rose in a deafening outburst of cheers and applause as he declared:

> The magnates and warlords of the Caribbean media are about to start yet another campaign against Grenada. While the Jamaican *Daily Gleaner*'s Hector Wynter travels to Trinidad to plan strikes with his fellow *Trinidad Guardian* and *Express* bloodsuckers, his compatriot and twin brother in lies and hypocrisy, Ken Gordon, is in Jamaica shamelessly announcing yet another plan of orchestrated propaganda destabilization against our Revolution.
>
> It seems that these clowns do not yet understand that the game is up, that they have been fully exposed before the Caribbean people and before their own workers, who so valiantly stood up to them in September and condemned them for their dishonesty and vulgarity, after their front-page fiasco.
>
> It seems that these Judases, who are willing to trade the journalistic integrity of their own workers and the limited value of their own depraved souls for just a few dollars more, are in need of yet another slap on their bottoms from the workers of the Caribbean.
>
> Let them continue to attack. The more they do so, the more they help the cause of the working people. For they are the best possible proof of the decadence, corruption and nasty stench of unmitigated, free enterprise capitalism, and its twin sister of rotting, hypocritical, saltfish journalism.[39]

A week later, the celebrated Barbadian novelist, George Lamming, in his address to the Forty-Second Conference of the Trinidad Oil Workers' Trade Union, spoke of the press tirade and conspiracy against Grenada. Referring in particular to the *Trinidad Guardian*, the *Express*, the Barbados *Advocate* and the Jamaica *Daily Gleaner*, he said: 'These national papers are not concerned with human rights or even press freedom. Their assignment is to destroy, by any means possible, the Government of Grenada'.

Biological Destabilization

In 1981 the Cuban representative of his Government told an official United Nations forum of its belief that the CIA were responsible for the epidemic of dengue fever, which had arrived in Cuba, and then moved southwards through the Caribbean, also reaching Grenada. The disease is spread by the Aedes Egypti mosquito, and can be fatal — as it proved in Cuba, where it caused 113 deaths. Cuba's case was reinforced by the publication of an article in the bi-monthly magazine of the Science Research Centre in the USA, *Science for the People*, which disclosed that contrary to a ban on such weapons, 'a CIA project still maintained stocks of biological warfare agents', and they had been applied against Cuba at the time of the 1962 Missile Crisis, then subsequently in 1971 when a deadly swine virus killed half a million pigs. The journal went on to say that 'during the past two years, Cuba has seen plant blights decimate its sugar, tobacco and coffee crops', and that the US base at Guantanamo on the Cuban mainland offered the CIA possibilities of a very useful launching pad for the introductions of such weapons.[40]

Grenada's Ministry of Health, through regular 'fogging' of vulnerable areas of mosquito breeding, plus a successful mobilization of vast sections of the population for mass community clean-ups of undergrowth, drains, culverts and any receptacles or pools of stagnant water where the mosquitoes could breed, managed to thwart the dengue with only a few cases being reported — but of course, the scare and the fear of the epidemic had been successfully sown.

Then, just a month later, another imported virus suddenly swept through the Caribbean in the wake of the dengue fever. This was 'haemorraghic conjunctivitis', better known as 'red eye' because of its effect in causing the infected eye to swell, turn red, burn and itch. Thousands of cases were reported in Cuba, thus causing tens of thousands of working hours to be lost, as sufferers found themselves unable to go to work often for an entire week. Again, the hidden hand of the CIA was suspected as the logical cause. The Pan-American Sanitary Office informed Cuba on 20 August that for the first time in history this disease had broken out in the hemisphere, reporting incidences in Suriname, Honduras and Colombia. The Cuban daily newspaper, *Granma*, pointed out that 'strangely, the disease has also appeared in our country, even though we have no exchange of personnel with these nations'.[41]

In Grenada people suffered from 'red eye' for many weeks, learning the lessons of biological destabilization with a great deal of physical irritation and the consequent loss of production. But the irrepressible humour of the people often turned it

to positive and collective effect — as in a Workers' Parish
Council in the town of Grenville on the East Coast, when
retired primary school principal and poet, Renalph Gebon,
recited his poem 'Red Eyes' to the joy and uproar of the
assembly. For whatever imperialism slings at Grenada, the
people have an answer:

> Eyes!
> Eyes!
> Eyes!
> Yes I's!
> Pearl has pearly eyes
> Jeanette has jealous eyes
> Sybil has sexy eyes,
> What's your eyes?
> I have
> Red eyes,
> Yes I's!
> I have
> Red eyes!

Destabilization using Religion and the Churches

Grenadian society is traditionally very religious, its people
members of many Christian denominations, large and small,
but with the Catholic Church being the most populous, followed by the Anglican, Methodist and Presbyterian. Being
members of these churches, however, has in no way prevented
Grenadians from also being active participants in and supporters of the Revolution. The People's Revolutionary Government has always adopted a generous and co-operative attitude
towards the Churches, particularly in the area of education,
where the relationship has been described by Prime Minister
Bishop as a 'partnership':

> Our record has been and our position today continues to be one of
> total co-operation, duty free concessions, help in fixing church
> property, help in fixing church schools, full and prompt payments
> of government grants to church schools, regular meetings between
> the Prime Minister and church leaders on a wide range of issues
> when the discussions have been frank, free, cordial and construc-
> tive, total freedom of religious worship, complete support for
> religious education in schools and so on.

This situation is very different from Gairy's vulgarity before the churches. While parading his Christian devotion, he had circulated prints of his own photograph to the priests and asked that they be placed prominently in the churches. Then, with an attitude of divine rectitude, he had taken indignant exception when ministers of various churches had refused to read out to their congregations his egocentric prayers, and had offended many Grenadians by proclaiming from the parliamentary chamber itself that 'he who opposes me, opposes God'. In 1973, after Catholic Bishop Patrick Webster had demanded an investigation into the Bloody Sunday outrage and the Church itself had played a prominent organizational part in forming the 'Committee of 22', which represented a strong and broad 'non-political' opposition to the dictator, Gairy had succeeded in pressurizing the Church hierarchy into transferring Webster out of Grenada.

During mid-February 1980, documents came into the possession of the People's Revolutionary Government that revealed how a small group of Catholic priests of the Dominican Order, were plotting to use Grenada as a test-bed for church agitation in a 'marxist-oriented society'. An intercepted letter from a Grenada-based priest to a colleague in England laid bare the intentions of this clique. Grenada was to become a workshop where certain reactionary elements of the Catholic Church would experiment in religious destabilization. The letter was very instructive:

Dear Jonathan,
   As the English Provincial Chapter approaches we would like to put a very serious proposal to you.
   The political situation in Grenada is developing rapidly. The island is becoming politically isolated within the English-speaking Caribbean as an object of fear to all other territories which, like Trinidad and Barbados, aspire to the ideology and lifestyle of the Western capitalist bloc. It is also attracting a great deal of attention in the diplomatic services of Britain and the USA.
   Within Grenada whatever political ideas may be entertained by the handful of people responsible for the People's Revolutionary Government (PRG) are becoming submerged under a massive Cuban influence. Cuba, Angola, Ethiopia, Vietnam and Kampuchea are now upheld as the models of development of a Third World State. Grenada was the only Caribbean state to vote with

Cuba against the UN resolution on the invasion of Afghanistan. A large number of young people have taken up university scholarships in Cuba. The Government is exercising more and more control over the dessemination of news and information. The great majority of the people are completely behind the Government in their aspirations to construct a new society, independent of American and all European influence in which they hope to discover their identity as a people (as Caribbean people).

The place of Christianity in this new vision remains problematic. There is a good deal of atheist indoctrination especially in the Army. It is only too easy to caricature the religion of the White God as one more colonial imposition which is, at best, irrelevant to Caribbean aspirations. But the population as a whole remains deeply attached to Christianity and the Government is trying hard to show that it has no quarrel with the Church. But the ultimate aim may well be to reduce it to a harmless and irrelevant organisation for children and old people and towards this end they are able to draw on twenty years of Cuban experience.

Faced with this situation the Bishop and Clergy are in disarray. There is a lack of any common analysis of the situation and of a common policy adjustment to it. We are out of our depth.

Over the last twenty years there has been much interest in Marxism among the brethren in England, and much talk about a Christian-Marxist dialogue. Many of the brethren are probably better read in modern Marxist ideology than any of the members of the PRG. Grenada offers them a tiny but significant field of experience in which to test out their theories and aspirations, an opportunity to preach the gospel in a predominantly Marxist-oriented society, while at the same time co-operating and assisting in the effort to construct a just human society. Grenada, therefore, poses an interesting challenge to English Dominicans, an opportunity to put theory into practice in a very small theatre of operations.

We would like you, therefore, to circulate this letter to all the brethren in the hope that three or four might feel called to respond to this challenge and help us to discover an effective way of preaching the gospel in a marxist situation for the building up of a strong local church and in forming a group of Caribbean Dominicans who will have to live and work in an increasingly Marxist Caribbean. The fact that they are English and white will certainly be against them, but for the moment it is no insuperable disadvantage. Their lack of knowledge about the local situation, of how people think and feel, need not hamper them for long. We have all had to learn this. There would be little difficulty, at present, about their entering the country to work as priests might be very different from that usually done in the area. There is great opportunities to influence the situation through preaching, adult education, youth work and perhaps even journalism — the church is planning to start a newspaper.

We make this appeal to you as we are assembled to further develop our plans for the future Caribbean province to emerge from our different vicariates in the region. As we consider the problem of what specific contribution, if any, a future Dominican province might make to the Church in the Caribbean — whether there is, in fact, any room for an order like ours to make a specific contribution — the problem of Grenada comes to our minds and the opportunities it offers for a very Dominican kind of work. But we have no men to begin with. We are persuaded that whatever happens in Grenada may have a profound effect on the work of the Church in the whole area.

The letter was disowned by Bishop Sydney Charles of St George's, who also agreed to withdraw the publication of the *Catholic Focus*, the journal referred to in the letter, under People's Law no 81, which forbad a newspaper company from publishing a newspaper if there are individuals in the company who own more than 4 per cent of the shares.

The letter formulated a particularly serious destabilization plan, as it threatened an intervention in an area which touched the hearts and emotions of many Grenadians, and the PRG lost no time in dealing with it. On 15 February the Prime Minister made a national broadcast, connecting the priests' conspiracy with other forms of political, economic and military destabilization that had taken place up to that point in time, and made the issue crystal clear to the population by reading the letter in full and analyzing the key passages. He also revealed that a number of anti-government tracts had been distributed from the same source as the letter, and that there was a clear offensive being launched to suggest that the PRG was trying to smother religious freedom in the country. A further letter was read and repudiated, from the 'Life-Study Fellowship' of Connecticut, USA, distributors of religious literature, which declared that they were being prevented from sending their texts to their subscribers in Grenada by 'government regulations' of the PRG.

The Government's position was clarified nationally in the same speech: 'Our people look to their church for spiritual guidance and to their Government for political leadership and we believe that this separation of Church and State is correct. . . . We repeat again our fullest commitment to freedom of worship and religion. We make this a permanent, standing commitment — now and forever.'

This incident was the single most serious attempt to use religion or the church to interfere with the process of the Revolution. Disaffected individuals have sometimes sought to use the church as their political pulpit. Alister Hughes, for example, at the 1982 Dominican Freedom Party convention, called upon the Grenadian churches to take the oppositional lead to the Revolution, and the Methodist minister Keith Ledson refused to conduct either the memorial service to Marryshow or the funeral service to McGodden 'Cacademo' Grant in November and December 1982 respectively, despite the fact that these were both national Heroes of Grenada. In both these instances, and in other isolated cases where individual priests have preached against parishioners joining the Militia, the voice of the most indignant and militant Grenadians has come from within the congregations themselves, who have told such priests in no uncertain terms to leave the Revolution alone and get on with their ecclesiastical business.

The real message of the majority of Christian Grenadians has frequently been voiced through the words of organizations like the Catholic Youth Congress. At their fifth annual convention, for example, having chosen their theme 'Education for Organization and Participation', they also produced their own songbook, combining both Christian and revolutionary enthusiasm in a determination to transform their nation and show how active and real their ideals are:

> We are great, great, great Christian workers
> and we're working all over the world,
> Yes, if everyone will join with us
> We'd surely bring imperialism down!

PART 3: NO BACKWARD REACTION COULD STOP OUR REVOLUTION!

RIGHT FROM the first weeks of the Revolution, the People's Revolutionary Government has continuously been alert to the dangers of destabilization in all its myriad forms and has at all times striven to pass on its insights to the Grenadian people. There must be no secrets from them, their security and the continued survival and advance of the Revolution depend upon it. In his speech of 8 May 1979, just weeks after the seizure of power, the Prime Minister revealed the advice given to him by a 'leading economist and advisor to several governments, who has very close contacts with individuals in the US State Department. He advised us that he had received information from his contacts inside the State Department that the Central Intelligence Agency had drawn up a plan to turn back the Grenada Revolution.' Bishop went on to explain that the plan had been conceived in the shape of a pyramid:

> At the bottom of the pyramid was a plan to destabilize the country by planting false reports about Grenada in newspapers and on radio stations, and also encouraging prominent individuals, organizations and governments in the region to attack our Revolution.
>
> The first part of the plan was aimed at creating dissatisfaction and unrest among our people and at wrecking the tourist industry and economy. A second level of the pyramid involved the use of violence and arson in the country. And if neither of these two methods worked in destabilizing the country, then the plan was to move to the stage of assassinating the leadership of the country.

Such explanations show clearly that the People's Revolutionary Government recognizes that only if the people themselves have all the facts presented to them seriously and unsparingly, can they begin to understand the real dimensions of destabilization.

For in Grenada the struggle against destabilization is minute-by-minute, day-by-day, week-by-week, beating back rumours and false statements, imported lies and slanders and provocative falsehoods being made by imperialist-cultivated, disaffected internal elements. This is the way destabilization can be fought, by a growth in popular consciousness and vigilance — and this is why the truth of the slogan is so exigent: 'A united, conscious, organized, vigilant people can never be defeated'. The leadership cannot oppose destabilization on its own or on behalf of the people, it can only oppose it with their full understanding and participation. Hence the mass activity and education around the topic and the high level of popular awareness of its functions and designs. This concern for the permament education of the people has been given even greater emphasis in 1983, which has been formally called 'The Year of Political and Academic Education'. The overall objective is to make the country and Revolution 'a big and popular school'.

For when there are international conferences designed to struggle against the efforts of the US to divide Grenada from the rest of the region and the world — whether it is the Socialist International Conference, the Conference of Workers of the Caribbean Basin of January 1981, the consecutive Caribbean Trade Union Conference and Grenada Solidarity Conference of November 1981 or the Conference of Lawyers and Conference of Caribbean Journalists of April 1982 — the masses are always involved automatically during public sessions, formal openings, receptions and radio broadcasts. When a delegation of Trinidadian journalists visited the country in December 1981 to find out for themselves about press and popular freedom in Grenada — or when any visitor answers the call of the People's Revolutionary Government to 'Come see for yourself!' — the Grenadian masses are the best and most conscious repulsers of the lies of imperialism. Thus the Trinidad journalists could return to their homeland and give a totally opposite view of Grenada to the Trinidadian people from their bosses' editorials. Without a 'united, conscious, organized and vigilant people' defending their country from systematic abuse and reaction, the destabilizers would have already won in Grenada.

It is those same iron qualities that have caused so many Grenadians to take the concrete and decisive step of joining the voluntary People's Revolutionary Militia and swear that 'not a grain of sand shall we yield to imperialism!', or simply to sing in the streets, as you will hear in Grenada, 'let them come, let them come, we go bury them in the sea!' The determined support given to 'The Heroes of the Homeland' manoeuvre of August 1981 was a clear declaration of faith in the Revolution and showed that anti-imperialism had entered into the very fibre of the people. The popular vocabulary arising from that consciousness was spontaneously expressed in the final weeks of 1981, when a lingering and unusually debilitating 'flu epidemic was hitting the population. The illness was soon labelled 'the manoeuvre' because it stayed around so long. Why? Because in Grenada everybody knows 'the manoeuvre will never over!'

Mass Mobilization with Mass Education

> It is one thing to prepare against an attack by a band of cowardly mercenaries sent by Eric Gairy. It is easy to recognize this kind of enemy. But destabilization is a different kind of enemy. It is much more subtle and much more deceptive. But it has a great weakness, a fatal flaw. Destabilization can only work when it goes unrecognized — like a thief in the night. Destabilization can work only when the people do not know that it is happening.
>
> It is a total failure when it is exposed — and when the people see it for what it is. The people of Grenada must learn what this destabilization is — because then we cannot be fooled by it.[42]

The mass mobilization of the people throughout Grenada has always been accompanied by mass formal and informal political education. In addition to Workers' Education classes in workplaces throughout the nation, through speeches, rallies, panel discussions, leaflets, newspapers and radio programmes, the danger of destabilization and the various stock-in-trade of the enemies of the Revolution have been discussed, considered, mulled over and internalized. They can then be reseminated, often pungently and humorously, through the cultural forms that have been given a new vibrancy through a revolutionary inspiration and content. In early 1981, for example, rumours were being orchestrated through Grenada by false reports from Radio Antilles, saying that a Cuban boat lying in St George's outer harbour and awaiting repairs to its engine, was in fact filled with the bodies of dead Grenadian soldiers who had been killed while fighting with the revolutionary forces in El Salvador. This

macabre rumour took on even more ghoulish whispers as it
spread, saying that there were up to two hundred dead soldiers
and they were being buried at night, five at a time. It was only
when a message from Major Gahagan, an officer in the People's
Revolutionary Army who was alleged to be among the dead,
was transmitted over Radio Free Grenada, that the rumour was
well and truly crushed:

> This is Major Basil 'Ackee' Gahagan speaking. I would like every-
> body in Grenada to know that I am alive and well and in good
> health. I am not sick and I am not dead. I want everybody to know
> that I have never been to El Salvador, and that although our country
> is internationalist in outlook, we have never interfered in the
> internal problems of other states, and therefore none of our soldiers
> have ever been to fight in El Salvador.

Soon after that, Sam Kee, an organizer of the Brizan Agricultural Co-operative and popular calypsonian, composed his
calypso 'Heavy Manners', which quickly became a nationwide
favourite:

> Cecilia come from the country
> Cecilia come down home by me
> Cecilia tell everybody how civil servant
>   on a go-slow,
> Heavy manners, Cecilia heavy manners!
>
> She say 'the dead on the boat
> Sam Kee, that ent no joke,'
> Heavy manners, Cecilia heavy manners!
>
> She say 'one thousand Cuban
> just arrive at the airport,'
> Heavy manners, Cecilia heavy manners!
>
> Cecilia mouth like a mule
> And she spreading bad news,
> Heavy manners, Cecilia heavy manners!
>
> Cecilia have she whole family
> Cecilia come down home by me
> Cecilia tell everybody how they
>   kill Gahagan,
> Heavy manners, Cecilia heavy manners!

What is wrong with Cecilia?
I want them to lock up Cecilia!
Cecilia have no respect for the law
            of this country,
Heavy manners, Cecilia heavy manners!

Cecilia mouth like a basket
Cecilia don't keep no secret,
Cecilia tell everybody how they
            kill Gahagan,
Heavy manners, Cecilia Heavy manners!

This was the best possible way of tackling the question of rumour-mongering, for it was coming directly from the masses to the masses. As Bishop made clear in a national broadcast on 18 September 1979, rumour-mongering may be the most mundane and unwitting, yet the most pernicious form of internal destabilization:

Sometimes we take rumours for granted and dismiss them as the innocent pastimes of idle people, and sometimes, of course, this is true. But we must never forget that rumours can be, and often are, used in a systematic and scientific way by our enemies as a method of spreading confusion, creating fear and panic and deteriorating and destroying the image of our government and its leadership.

Let us consider some examples. The early rumour that I had been bitten by a bee and was no longer able to see was meant to suggest that Gairy's mystical and *obeah* qualities had begun to work on me, and was clearly an appeal to the backward and superstitious beliefs of some of our people. The later rumour, that my colleague and brother, Comrade Bernard Coard, had cuffed me, was meant to suggest that there were serious divisions in the leadership of the party and government, and that a power struggle was taking place.

In particular, the nature and role of the CIA, as the fountain-head of lies and imperialist intrigue, has been identified as a major part of the people's curriculum against destabilization. The lessons of Chile and Guyana have been learned at mass rallies in solidarity with the Chilean people and visits by Dr Cheddi Jagan, ex-Prime Minister of Guyana and victim of British colonial repression and direct intervention during the 1950s and 1960s. In September 1980, John Stockwell, an ex-CIA agent in Angola, toured Grenada giving the people many insights into the venomous methods of his ex-bosses, and in July–August 1981, Philip Agee, now travelling on a Grenadian passport, also visited Grenada and spoke at various meetings of mass organizations and rallies throughout the country. With their enormous capacity for permanent education, the Grenadian people listened carefully to these authorities on the workings of their principal enemy, and learned well. So well, in fact, that when two more ex-CIA officers — Bill Schaap and Ralph McGehee — came to the country in August 1982, they acknowledged at a press conference that 'you know more about the CIA in Grenada than many in the USA, including the average college graduate'.

The Centre For Popular Education

> Destabilizer brainwash the illiterate
> But this time they will be too late,
> For when they are ready to attack
> We'll be ready to send them back!

> *Gillian Gordon*[43]

While destabilization is one of the realities that Grenadians must sleep and wake with, it is bound to be a part of the unconscious and conscious knowledge of the people. The Centre for Popular Education (CPE), which is the national literacy and adult education structure, recognized this truth, and from its inception brought into its theme lessons the need to be vigilant. In fact, the letter 'V' was taught through the literacy manual using the statements: 'To keep our freedom we must be vigilant. We must defend our villages and country. A viligant militia in every village.'[44] And opposite these boldly printed words is a dramatic photograph of some armed Militia members in a jeep. Unit Six in the Adult Education Manual, which teaches the uses of nouns, quotes a passage describing the counter-revolutionary murders in St Patrick's in November 1980. Its last sentence reads: 'Acts of counter-revolution teach us in a painful way who the enemy is. Such brutal acts cannot intimidate us. They make us more determined. When a forceful and determined people cry, injustice trembles.'[45]

Later on in the course, an extract from Bishop's 'In Nobody's Backyard' speech becomes the base text to teach the past continuous tense. There is nothing forced or unnatural in using such material. It is a true reflection of what is actually happening in the country, a barometer of the pressure of the times in Grenada that must be linked with the need to be able to read and write, to be able to rationalize, to absorb and understand, to be able to make choices, as people are doing every day in Grenada. Then, as has been stressed many times by Bishop: 'it will be so much easier for our people not to be misled, and to understand more and more what is happening in their country, their region and their world. It will be so much easier for them to understand this word we use so often — *imperialism* — it will be so much easier for them to understand what we mean when we talk of *destabilization.*'[46]

The First Phase of the Centre for Popular Education which ended in February 1981, proved to be a genuine success. Not only because of its record in creating literacy amongst those who had almost given up hope of ever being able to read and write, and building a much needed confidence amongst the hundreds of mainly young volunteer teachers, but also because it mobilized people through its cultural events and emulation sessions and created a dynamic sense of popular unity around the question of *permanent* education, making people more and more aware of their own situation and that of their country in relation to the rest of the region and the world. In doing this it created new cadres, new consciousness, new forms of collective organization and study. While Ronald Reagan was conceiving his CBI plan over the heads of the masses of the region, Grenada was building on its CPE plan to make its people fully conscious under the slogan, 'Each one teach one, let us learn together. No liberation without Education!' Teacher-poet Renalph Gebon put this plan into his own characteristic words:

CPE PLAN

Brother man;
CPE plan,
Dat each one
Go teach one,
So we go 'ave
Ah better lan.

        Who know,
        Go show,

Who en know,
How to know,
Wah e doh know.

High or low,
E go know,
How go grow,
Peas an potato,
Calalloo and ochro.

E go learn to make,
Conkie and fishcake,
Even bread an bakes,
E go weave basket,
For dee market.

E go learn to read
And know how to write,
Mal-joe e go cure,
And learn to sew,
Crab e go hold;
Ball e go bowl.
Fish e go catch;
And for watch,
And let bullet pass
If they cut across.

Brother man;
We go go,
Hand in hand
Working, hands an head
To get a daily bread.

Dah is the plan,
Dee C.P.E. plan,
Brother man.[47]

Workers' Education

Dear Comrade,

The Ministry of National Mobilization is pleased to extend a special invitation to you, to attend the up-coming one-and-a-half-hour weekly series of *Worker Education Classes* which will be conducted *right at your workplace.*

No doubt you may have already heard about this new and exciting programme and may want to know a bit more about what is in store for you and your fellow comrades. Well, this is part of the surprise.

However, it is sufficient to say that the *Worker Education Classes* will answer and inform comrades on questions like: Why is our country poor? Are there no *social classes* in Grenada, and if there are classes to which social class do the workers belong? Will there always be rich and poor? Why must we as workers try to produce more? When were our trade unions formed and for what reasons? Have there always been trade unions? And finally, how does our economy work? And much, much more.

Comrade, this programme is intended for all workers, and it is about workers. See you at the classes.

> *Letter of invitation to workers for*
> *Workers' Education Classes,* August 1981

We need to look back and watch we own lives and work and study weself. Is knowledge we after. It have plenty brain between we, but it shy to come up.

> *Dockworker,* March 1982

Another example of the new and permanent concentration upon education in Grenada which now contributes to awareness of the drive for progress, and the dangers of regress and destabilization, are the Workers' Education Classes that take place on a regular basis at workplaces throughout the nation. During these sessions the last thirty years of Grenada's history are scrutinized, analyzed and discussed, using common material but with the experiences of the participants very much a vibrant part of the syllabus. By studying events beginning from the 1951 Agricultural Workers' rebellion in Grenada which swept Gairy into power, and his subsequent betrayal of the same workers through his despotic rule and corrupt union, to the 1973–74 upsurge against Gairyism and the sell-out by the trade union leadership when the workers had the knife at the Dictator's throat, through the formation of the New Jewel Movement and the struggles of the 1970s until the Revolution of 1979 — workers can analyze the forces of progress and those who sought to hold it back, and apply those lessons to the regional and world situation and the present period of imperialist destabilization. The definition of the enemy becomes much clearer through these classes and they have done much to sharpen both the confidence and the political awareness of Grenada's working people. 'Thy consciousness shall be thy guide', sings the Flying Turkey in his calypso 'No More Shackles', and the people's consciousness is what is being transformed, above all, through this mass offensive of education taking place throughout the country at so many different levels.

These classes, combined with the 'People's Budget', in which the entire population of the country is involved in continuing pre-budget consultation and education procedures, with discussion, analysis, the raising of suggestions and criticism taking place at workplaces, Parish and Zonal Councils and trade union meetings — as well as conferences for delegates of the mass organizations and their own village and parish groups — have caused an extraordinary growth in understanding of the national and world economic systems, and the causes of the poverty and continuous economic destabilization that countries such as Grenada suffer. This new awareness come out sharply in the lyrics of the calypsoes of the first carnival after such a Budget procedure, in 1982. King Shy of the African Temple calypso tent, was clearly well towards fathoming the system in his calypso, 'Rip-off':

> I am fed up, tell me when this thing go stop,
> About them oppressive boys who calling themself big-shot.
> While them kind ah fellas relaxing
> We catching we tail producing,
> And our products man, they buying it for nothing.
> When they send it back to us in bottle, tins and so —
> With big prices to kill the poor.

> CHORUS: *You see, when we work so hard*
> *Tell me who getting the benefit?*
> *The capitalists, the imperialists.*
> *When we grow we crops*
> *Tell me who fixing the price for it?*
> *The capitalists, the imperialists.*
> *Tell me when they send we goods for we*
> *Who fixing the price for it?*
> *The capitalists, the imperialists.*

> I can't understand, yes, what's going on:
> When they send their goods for we, they fixing the price for it.
> Still when we grow we crops
> Man, the prices they have to fix.

And their prices so dread man, they really killing the poor.
And the fellas have no mercy —
Look what they doing to countries like we.
But for those who love to exploit, we go finally put things right.

In thunder and lightning, man we have to be working,
Then them boys step in and we they start commanding.
With excess goods from up there
To we they introduce,
And they don't care whether the region depends on them,
But they say we have to do it, because all we cannot keep.

Those who want a cutlass to buy them have to catch their ass,
For to get it, we have to pass hard dollars,
Export competitive goods prices are below low,
Yet that don't move them because they have no regards for the poor,
But I say they will never get away!

Rallies

The Rally is certainly an assembly which combines mass mobilization with mass education and, as utilized by the Grenada Revolution, is clearly a device which contributes to fighting destabilization. From their earliest days of resistance to the Gairy dictatorship, the New Jewel Movement recognized both their usefulness and their essential appeal to the people. For their first great rally, the People's Convention, in 1973, they attracted 15,000 people, and this popular tradition now continues in the form of mass assemblies to commemorate significant national anniversaries and also to show solidarity with many of the struggling peoples of the world — from South Africa and Namibia to Vietnam, from the Western Sahara to El Salvador.

On the anniversary of the fascist coup in Chile in September 1980, the People's Revolutionary Government organized two rallies simultaneously in different parishes of the country to emphasize to the people — using the example of Chile — the dangers of imperialist interference in the Revolution. In the north of the nation at Sauteurs, Prime Minister Bishop and George Lamming made speeches highlighting the continued attempts of the CIA to obstruct the Revolution. Lamming emphasized, in particular, the importance of culture and literacy being at the heart of the Revolution to give it health and vibrancy, and stressed that the development of new democratic institutions was crucial for organizing the people and ensuring their constant participation. Bishop demonstrated the lessons that must be learned from Chile: 'The Chilean Revolution failed because it lacked this last fundamental principle; that of controlling the military power in the country and arming the people.'[48]

Meanwhile, in the southernmost part of the island in the Parish of St David's Deputy Prime Minister Coard was comparing the situation in Chile in 1973 with that in Jamaica as he spoke. In pointing to the influence of the CIA and its grip upon *El Mercurio* in Chile and *The Daily Gleaner* in Jamaica, Coard reminded the assembly that the CIA had a year's supply of newsprint in Miami, waiting to be shipped to *The Torchlight* at the time that it was closed down: 'If we don't organize ourselves, the CIA will organize us!' he declared.

This proximity to the people continually demonstrated by the PRG ministers means that they are always talking to the people, always listening to them, always organizing with them. The Grenadian people see their ministers everywhere and are constantly informed and involved in decisions taken on major and minor national events. An example of this was in April 1981, when Coard was fighting a diplomatic struggle in Brussels to win support and secure funding for the new international airport from the EEC, a massive movement for support for the airport was building up inside Grenada, behind the slogan 'Our new international airport unites the people!'. In the week immediately before the rally at the airport site which drew 12,000 people, the Prime Minister personally visited forty-three workplaces to talk to the workers and farmers and listen to their views on the project.

The massive attendance at the rally was the direct result of that closeness with the people. As Bishop told the crowd, 'Today we show the world that we have decided to build our international airport, regardless of who vex!', an army of banners and placards were raised to the sky, all of them talking back: 'Hands off imperialism!' 'This land belongs to us!', 'Long live the Revo, we want our Airport!', 'We too know the importance of our International Airport!', 'Our Airport means building our country!' and 'God bless our PM, I am a strong supporter!' It was proof that it was not just a listening experience, but an emergent form of people's participation in the life of the young country. For when Coard returned a few days' later with the triumphant

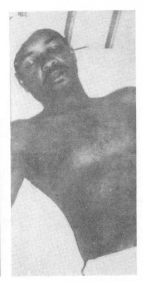

. Exchange of gifts: Gairy and President Pinochet of Chile.
. Victims of Bloody Sunday, November 18th 1973: Maurice Bishop, Selwyn Strachan, Unison Whiteman.

3. Funeral of Rupert Bishop: January 1974.
4. The people vs. Gairy: January 1974.

Maurice Bishop, Prime Minister of Grenada.

6. Cheddi Jagan in Grenada, 1981.
7. Michael Manley in Grenada, 1983, Richard Hart in background.

8. Weapons and documents on display, seized from counter-revolutionary conspirators: June 1980.

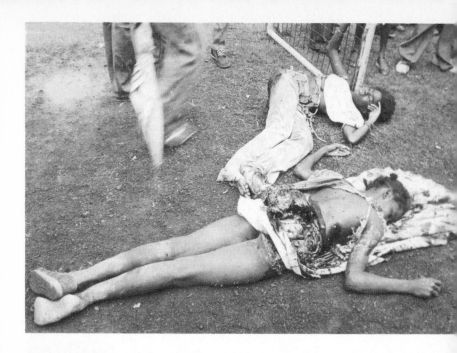

9. June 19th 1980: the victims.

10. The message to counter-revolutionaries.

REVOLUTION HAS NO ROOM FOR
TERRORIST
JOIN THE MILITIA NOW AND
FIGHT TERROR

Long live the memory
of Salvador Allende

The day after the St. Patrick's murders, November 1980: schoolchildren take to the streets in protest.

Rally in solidarity with the people of Chile, September 1980. A pioneer addresses the meeting. George Lamming and
an Ambassador Julian Rizo listen.

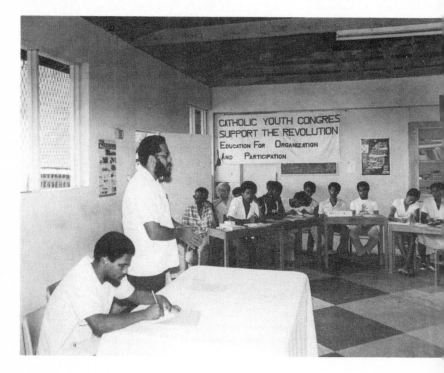

13. Demonstration, June 19th (Heroes' Day) 1981.

14. Deputy Prime Minister Bernard Coard addresses a seminar of the Catholic Youth Congress.

15. Trade Union Unity: Workers' March, May 1st 1981.
16. Workers' Education class at the Woodlands Sugar Factory.

17. Billboard: Grenville.
18. The People's Militia: ever vigilant.

The People's Militia: 'The manoeuvre will never be over!'
A group of C.P.E. volunteers.

21. The Grenadian people, united and resolute: Bloody Sunday, 1982.

22. Demonstration outside the residence of one of the sponsors of 'The Grenadian Voice', June, 1981.

support package, the people's involvement was intensified by being fully informed about every detail of the negotiations. Imperialist diplomatic and propaganda destabilization had backfired upon itself, not only externally, but internally too. Far from dividing the people, the issue further consolidated national unity, with all the trade unions, the Chamber of Commerce and the Lawyers' Society — as well as mass organizations like the National Women's Organization (NWO), the National Youth Organization (NYO) and the National Students' Council (NSC), all firmly behind the Revolution's largest capital project to date.

Structures of Revolutionary Democracy

i: Workers' Parish Councils and Zonal Councils

In June 1981 the People's Revolutionary Government established the Ministry of National Mobilization, with Selwyn Strachan as Minister. This was a further manifestation of the maxim in revolutionary Grenada that 'Organization is our greatest weapon', and that the more the people exist in organized relationships with each other behind the Revolution, the safer the Revolution is from being destabilized. One of the first aims of this unique new ministry was to devise accountability structures for the mass of the people, whereby they could call to account officials, high-ranking civil servants and the managers of State enterprises and also the ministers themselves, if they were unsure or dissatisfied about their performance, while also using the councils as mechanisms for putting forward their own contributions, suggestions, criticism and views on all aspects of national and social development.

The Zonal Councils began as parishwide assemblies, but soon attendance and participation became so great that they split into *Zonal* Councils, representing zones or clusters of villages in any particular parish. These community-based structures were complemented by worker-based assemblies, organized through trade unions and workers' committees and called Workers' Parish Councils. Now both organs are flourishing and regular, vibrant components of Grenada's revolutionary democracy. As such they play an important role in consolidating the unity of the people, gelling the spirits of all who meet in

democratic resolve to push forward their Revolution together.
As calypsonian Mighty Awful sings in his 'Freedom Train':

> Steady comrades steady, mind there!
> No dictator, no way,
> We are free at last
> Not as in the past,
> Forward ever,
> Backward never,
> Mass mobilisation
> Pushing the struggle on,
> Who trying, trying in vain
> To stop the freedom train!

At the councils the people present are frequently informed
about the situation outside the country through an address by
one of the ministers which brings the evening to a close. While
the US armed forces were playing out the dress rehearsal of
an invasion of Grenada during the 'Ocean Venture '81'
manoeuvres off Vieques, Prime Minister Bishop addressed the
St George's Workers' Parish Council, after the necessary
accountability procedures with the Manager of the Electricity
Company had been completed, a new Rent Restriction Act had
been read and discussed in detail, and the Council's wishes for
a national bus service had been received and hearkened to. The
speech from the Prime Minister was received tumultuously
after he gave detailed information about the US military
destabilizations in the Caribbean, and also reminded those
present to increase their democratic will and put themselves
day by day into a more organized relationship with all aspects
of the Revolution.[50]

ii: The Mass Organizations

The National Women's Organization and the National Youth
Organization are mass structures rooted in the struggles of the
Grenadian people against the Gairy dictatorship. The integra-
tion and growing involvement of both women and youth in the
revolutionary process has been one of the most effective means
of organizing against internal destabilization. In 1981, the year
of the greatest threat so far to the Revolution, the 'Ocean
Venture '81' manoeuvres, the National Women's Organiza-

tion, with its determined and widely internalized slogan, 'Women equal in production and defence', quadrupled its membership from 1,300 at the beginning of the year by the time of the end of their emulation campaigns during the final months of the year. Over the same period the National Youth Organization also quadrupled its membership.

The mass organizations knit into each other and overlap in many of their functions and activities. A young woman, for example, might be a member of the NYO, the NWO, a local Party Support Group and the Militia. She might also be active in her trade union. Thus the cultural, sporting, educational, defence and recreational activities of each would have their effect on dynamizing participation in the others, until the sister was involved in a many-faceted and connected series of organized relationships with her peers and fellow Grenadians that would make her a very formidable citizen indeed, with more social force and levels of personal and social organization than most people in the so-called 'developed' societies. Such a person, increased many thousand times, in rank after rank, is a hard opponent for any destabilizer.

iii: The Trade Unions

The Revolution has brought new freedoms to the Grenadian trade union movement. During the dictatorship, Gairy himself held the unions in a vice, by corrupting his own Grenada Manual and Mental Workers' Union from the head downwards, and alternately bribing and intimidating the leadership of the other unions. Many active trade unionists received the customary message at the time of impending militant action: 'If you strike, you dead!' The PRG has encouraged the development of a new, participatory and democratic trade union movement that is truly independent and vibrant, by laying the legal foundation for its creation and rapidly responding to workers' demands for better conditions, increased wages, maternity leave, an end to sexual discrimination by an equal pay for equal work decree, a national insurance scheme and mandatory profit sharing on both state and private estates.

During the Gairy years, the American Institute for Free Labor Development—trained trade union leaders operated in a way which was totally divorced from the mass of their membership. There was little or no accountability, few general meetings of the membership and thus a very low level of interest and participation. In the Technical and Allied Workers' Union, one of the full-time officials was even on an AIFLD wage, and thus indirectly employed by the CIA. His salary was funnelled to him through the Caribbean Congress of Labour. As one of his fellow Executive members said: 'They were his bosses over there in America, not us union members here in Grenada. You could see how dangerous this was, and the members didn't know about it, they were kept in the dark.' In several unions, including TAWU, so few members ever attended the general meetings that it proved impossible to make quorums.[51]

That kind of situation is now impossible in the trade unions of Grenada. In TAWU, for example, which is now under totally different leadership — the ex-president of the union left Grenada hastily a week after the Revolution — meetings are both regular and well-attended, the posts are elected, the books are open for the scrutiny of all members, procedures are democratic, weekly seminars are held on trade union practice and there has been an overwhelming increase in membership since the Revolution repealed all Gairy's anti-union laws and allowed workers to join the union of their choice. This new activity within the unions by the ordinary members soon exposed the backward leadership. The AIFLD plant in TAWU was the first to be exposed. As Fred Grant, founder member and trustee of the union explained: 'It took the Revolution to find out about him, but then we realised he was a CIA front man, and so he had to vacate his job.'

In the Public Workers' Union, the same Executive that called for the sick-out in March 1981 and appeared to be very militant against the People's Revolutionary Government had opposed militant action against Gairy. It was soon found by its own membership to be reluctant to have meetings and share its knowledge with its members, as well as being so incompetent that it couldn't organize its own elections. The narrow economism of its leadership saw trade unionism solely in terms of more and higher wage demands, excluding any concept of playing an active role in building the economy and the Revolution, as if its members, all participants in the State machinery, had no other function in a revolutionary situation. The union's younger members in particular, in forming the '12 November Committee' — named after the date of a giant unofficial meeting which they held to mobilize the membership to play a more active part in the affairs of the union — revolted against the existing Executive and won the majority of the membership over to productive policies after a massive opposition campaign and debate amongst the nation's public workers. The new thrust aimed to put the union right behind the revolutionary advance being made in Grenada, and saw the members contributing to all aspects of national development, rather than merely following the isolating and divisive 'white collar' approach of its leaders.

The democratic appetite of the Revolution has massively increased both membership and participation in the unions and blown away the old lethargy and corruption. The Bank and General Workers' Union has risen from just one hundred members in the banks to three thousand members in all walks of life, from hotels to garment factories to nutmeg receiving stations. The Commercial and Industrial Workers' Union has experienced a 50 per cent increase in membership, the Technical and Allied Workers' Union a 60 per cent increase. The Agricultural and General Workers' Union, a new union forged in the course of the Revolution, has grown to a membership of well over two thousand agricultural workers. This new trade union health and consciousness has clearly made the Grenada Trade Union Movement a much more difficult target for CIA penetration. The workers are active, vigilant and conscious, and seminars and sessions of political education at workplaces have increased their general understanding of the nature and forces of destabilization that have tried to infiltrate them and work through them in the past. Now the trade unions exist as a barrier against imperialist pressure, for the majority of their members realize that an honest government that finds whatever money it can for its workers and also builds a social wage for them, opens all its books for its workers and seeks participation from them in all major national, decisions including the formation of the budget, is also a force for protecting workers and hastening their advance and emancipation from the suffering of the past. Government and trade union movement are more and more side by side, and, when the US invasion rehearsal was threatening the country in August 1981, the Trades Union Council made its position very clear in a call for all trade unionists to register for the Militia and stand prepared to deal with any imperialist attack. From being something of a vulnerable underbelly for the destabilizers, the trade union movement in Grenada has now transformed itself, largely by its own inner momentum, to a firm line of defence against them.

The Media

The non-stop onslaught by the 'saltfish' press and imperialist radio network of the Caribbean against the Grenada Revolution has meant that the struggle against propaganda destabilization also has to be relentless. For a small, poor country with very limited media resources, Grenada sees its principal strategy in fighting the giant 'media monsters' as joining with other progressive, Third World and nonaligned nations around the world as a part of the international movement to create a New World Information Order. The main directions of this struggle are set out in Maurice Bishop's opening address to the First Conference of Journalists from the Caribbean Area, organized jointly by the International Organization of Journalists, the Federation of Latin American Journalists, the Press Association of Jamaica and Grenada's own Media Workers' Association of Free Grenada. That speech is included as an appendix to this work, and is so far the fullest statement of Grenada's struggle against propaganda destabilization and her strategies to deal with it.

Revolutionary Culture against Imperialist Destabilization

One of the results and continuing manifestations of the Grenada Revolution is its dynamic and highly original cultural movement. Popular culture is at the heart of the Revolution as it had been at the heart of the anti-Gairy struggle, and in particular, for the first time in an English-speaking country, we are seeing what happens to the English language in the midst of revolutionary transformation. For it is clear that the cultural forms flowing from the revolutionary determination and advances of the Grenadian people have introduced qualities and innovations that are unprecedented in the history of the language. English has never been so actively and profoundly the language of Revolution before, and now the language itself and the forms it embraces — in particular oral poetry and calypso — have also been integrated into the struggle against destabilization.

i: Oral Poetry

From being mainly an individualistic, private art form under colonialism, founded on mimicry of the writers of the colonial power, poetry has burst into the mainstream of revolutionary life in Grenada. Apart from its regular appearance in *The Free West Indian* and the other journals of the Revolution, poetry has become a regular feature of radio, rallies and Zonal and Parish Workers' Councils. These performances are not seen as tokenistic 'cultural breaks', but in every way integral to the urgency and necessity of whatever is being discussed, informed or commemorated.

The electric effect of poetry being read at a Workers' Parish Council, and seeing what was perverted for decades into an élitist form, come vibrating back into the popular consciousness I sought to describe in the opening chapter of *Is Freedom We Making*, in the description of that same St George's Workers' Parish Council at the time of the US manoeuvres off Vieques. The following three poems, all of which have been performed orally at mass events, show how Grenada's young poets are putting their skills right behind the struggle against destabilization, the major priority for all militants, including the writers and artistes. The poet of 'The Basin Plan', Michael 'Senator' Mitchell, is an immigration officer and performs his poems in the manner of African chants, accompanying himself upon a drum. Eighteen year-old Garvin Stuart is a journalist working for *The Free West Indian*. His 'Look All About' reflects the words and images on Militia posters all around the nation, warning the people to 'Look out — Imperialism never rests!' 'The Last Cowboy' was written by Chris 'Kojo' de Riggs, who apart from being one of his country's leading poets, is also the Minister of Health.

THE BASIN PLAN

CHANT: *No! No!*
No to the Basin Plan
No to the cunning plan
No to the mad-man plan
No to the dread-dread plan!

The Basin Plan
Beautiful Caribbean
Peaceful Caribbean
Strategic location
We want to suck you as a ligarou[52]
Leave you weak, meek, sick
Can't stand on your own feet
All your natural resources
We going to be bosses
Got big-big industries
Draining your economy
Leaving you hungry
Poverty, tears, misery
On bending knees
Committed to we
The big red apple
Ready as Freddie
Willing to supply all devices
Arms, Hawkers, bombers, missiles
Even fighters
Maccoo neutron[53]
Share tension in the region
Military manoeuvre take over
Aggressive expansion in the Caribbean

CHANT: *Prowling as a roaring lion*
Best Superman
Grabbing with an iron hand
Squeezing developing lands
Isolating progressive nation
Seeking to devour
In your own favour
United labour, people's power
Still causing disaster
Polluting the atmosphere
Constant fear
Spreading your tentacles
Here, there, everywhere
Like a giant octopus
Viciously grabbing
Without realising
The damage causing

Preaching peace
Yet the big whip, at your hip
Spanning nations behind
Ent care one damn
In full command
But the masses chant
No! No!
No to the Basin Plan
No to the cunning plan
No to the dread-dread plan
The Basin Plan yankee aggression
The Basin Plan want to smash the Caribbean
The Basin Plan corruption, confusion
The Basin Plan division of the land
The Basin Plan spreading waste all over
The place
Hate and disgrace —
Just wait.

LOOK ALL ABOUT

Look to the north,
the east and the west
also the south,
you go see crazymen in
Washington wearing a pout
cowboys riding nuclear rockets
out-of-control Wall Street puppets
and frenzied vampires screaming
for profits

Look to the north
the east and the west
also the south,
and you go see
yardfowl and mother hen
telling us don't defend
lackeys of the White House
with louse and mouse
as aides and maids,
with lice and mice
telling them they nice
as they scratch, crawl and shuffle

and meddle with vice.
Animals with rabies
marines, criminals and mercenaries
a latrine in a series.

Look to the north
the east and the west
also the south,
swell your chest
and kick them out!

Those dogs of war
that will kill
their own mothers for a twenty five cents
who trample and strangle
without relent.

Sharpen your cutlasses
hone your knives
deal with those asses
protect innocent lives
clean your rifle
load your magazine
they cannot stifle
a popular dream!

Grab your child
put the future on your shoulder
grab your woman
also hold a boulder
to knock them down
when they come around.
Grab a fork, grab a hoe
cry 'No more!'
to Yankee pigs
out to invade we shore.

So look to the north
for Lord Pentagon
dying in Washington
and Mistress CIA
getting spit in she face
day after day

with their nasty newborn
called Ugly Neutron
surnamed Killer Bomb.

Let them come
the sea is their grave
we is runaway slave
we is steel in fireside
red-hot *Amber and the Amberines*
prepared to burn down
all their latrines

So let them come
if they want Grand Anse
and Point Salines
to be stained with their stink blood
Let them come
we go bury them in the mud
and drown their dirtiness
in Freedom's flood.
Let Reagan and them
feel the weight of the AK
and know this Revolution
is here to stay!

Look to the north
the east and the west
let them know
we harder than the rest
and come what may
we will pass the test

Look to the south
when they show up
Militia pass them out!
For we children's future
Look all about!

THE LAST COWBOY

Ronald Reagan, the ageing cowboy bandit man
Cooked up a major bandit plan,
This man pattern, this comic clown

Of movie fame and bushwacking fun
Announced that he was riding down
Through his backyard and islands in the sun
To put more notches on his gun.
For Ronald Reagan 'twas not strange
To go gun-shooting on his range
To shoot back all dese winds of change.

So paff-paff Reagan wid face like twine
And Caribbean Basin in he mind,
Was determined to keep everybody in line
And all yuh rebel is land slaves
Resisting just like Indian braves
Will end up dead in rebel graves,
And all yuh natives playing rude
Look out — I'm in a looting, tooting, shooting mood.

'Just like in de movies,' he said to himself
As he removed his six-shooters from up on de shelf,
'I'll fight for America, yes I will
For America I'll die — kill, kill, kill!
For de big boys and dem up on Capitol Hill,
America de land of de free and de bold
We give you de land and take all de gold.

America must direct the course of humanity
And he who resists we kill with impunity,
We make de plans, we pass out de orders
We empty wash basins just outside we borders,
We direct bombings, assassinations and murders
We preach it in our school to our sons and our daughters —
These boys of the backyard are living in we waters.

So I'll attack like in days gone by,
Grenada go bawl and Cuba go cry,
And every other bugger is sure to die.
Like old McCarthy I'll go on a hunt
And mark up every piece a liberation front,
And Nicaragua must fall before end a mont' —
No matter who protest, don't bother who gripe
Dey all must bow down to de stars and stripes.'

And so this maniac, gunslinging clown
Stood ready to ride in and gun down the town,
Eventually to strike all humanity down —
A cowboy desperado with nuclear power
Threatening mankind hour after hour,
Trying vainly to stop the march of people's power.

ii: Calypso

False propaganda aimed at disaster
Spread by opposition and reactionary,
Only lies and accusations about my country.
While they are trying to give us a bad note
We are working to complete our airport,
Creating jobs and further education
Processing food and fish to feed the nation.
Recognise our stand,
'cause we control our own land.

So sang The Flying Turkey in his 'Voice of My People'. The chorus of that calypso became a national slogan on the lips of the people, and was to be heard being sung spontaneously at rallies, assemblies and even through the streets as steel bands took up the chorus in the 1981 Grenada Carnival:

No, no, no, Imperialism no!
No, no, no, Imperialism no!
No backward reaction could stop this Revolution!
No backward reaction could stop this Revolution!

This was a typical extension of Grenadian revolutionary culture that having come from the pulses of the people, passed directly back from the calypsonian into their lives and minds. Turkey's remarkable 'Innocent Blood', written to commemorate the 'deaths of all the heroes and martyrs who fall' in the struggle to build the new society, became one of the most regularly-played calypsoes on the radio, and the record was played throughout the island, touching the emotions of people who had lived through the 19 June bombings and the November murders. Turkey's expansion of the theme to the worldwide struggle against imperialism became another form of political education in a mass form. Grenada was ceasing to be merely a

small island, it was at one with the fight of the oppressed of the
world:

INNOCENT BLOOD

In a revolution some people are weak
While others are strong,
Listen to my song.
The weak turn to counter-revolution
Subversion and destabilization.
It's the strong ones to stand firm and make things right,
Show to the weak why we must unite.
The weak, them they don't know
Who they fighting for,
Moving aimlessly, in a senseless war,
Murdering their people
Innocent along the way,
But we are go whip them
So listen when I say.

They don't care about the children
In this here time,
They don't care about the children, oh no.
I say they preaching war,
Say what they kill them for?
Bernadette Laurice and Laureen.

In a revolution some people are right
While others are wrong,
Listen to my song.
The wrong always feel that they have it right,
That they are correct, so they want to fight.
It's the right ones to lead them and show them the way,
They get more confused each and every day.
Their opportunism and reaction too,
Show these our brothers, their dirty works to do
Turn them into robots, puppets on a string,
They kill their own sisters
And they don't care a thing.

In a revolution there will be progress
Pain, sorrow and fun,

Listen to my song.
The joy of the years will be mixed with tears
Bitter and sweet, as we move along.
The genuine ones stand firm to the end,
We understand that we must defend.
But in 1980, the Nineteenth of June,
Imperialism on that afternoon
Raised its cruel hands
And innocent blood get shed
And now Bernadette, Laurice and Laureen are all dead.

Look what they do to Alister
Tell me, what they do that for?
Alister blood was innocent blood
Rupert Bishop, he was innocent too.
I say, innocent blood spill in Angola
Innocent blood spill in Jamaica
Innocent blood spill in Havana
Innocent blood spill in Grenada
Innocent blood in Guatemala
Innocent blood in Nicaragua
Innocent blood in El Salvador
Innocent blood spill in Vietnam

Stop the tribal war
I tell you say, a war leaves scars,
The four people were going in a car
They pick up them gun and they open fire
I tell you say a murder on the land!
Black people, you should never, never fight
Sometimes, you know, you got to defend your rights
I say to go there with your tribal war.
You keep on shooting everybody down
I say you wouldn't see the rising sun.

Harold Strachan blood was innocent blood
Stanislaus blood was innocent blood
Walter Rodney blood was innocent blood
Steve Biko blood was innocent blood
Romero blood was innocent blood
Lalsee blood was innocent blood
Courtney blood was innocent blood
Evan Charles blood was innocent blood.[54]

Support for the new international airport united all the calypsonians, and many of them were becoming inspired to write and perform songs on this theme. The Mighty Guava sang that

> Now is the time for uniting
> Now is the time for re-arranging,
> Nor more hating, no more shooting,
> No more fighting but the time for building.

and he advised:

We are getting pressure from countries who think they are great,
But if we just stand firm one day we will go strong . . .

In his chorus he appealed to the people:

> Please don't let them stop us
> No don't let them stop,
> We must not fuss, 'cause when we fuss
> We will stay right in the dust,
> We have to see our airport carry on,
> We have to see the project work is done
> And at the end
> It will benefit all!

Lord Melody, another veteran calypsonian, sang in his 'Grenada Since the Revolution' that the airport itself was another great proof of the forward march of the Grenadian people:

> Since after the Revolution
> We have a change in every direction,
> Look around us and you will see
> The rise in our economy,
> It's a miracle, some people does say,
> Believe it or not we are on our way.
>
> CHORUS: *Grenada is moving fast*
> *We reaching somewhere at last,*
> *Our motto we must remember*
> *'Forward ever and backward never!'*
>
> Our international airport is striving,
> Although there is plenty talking
> How we shouldn't have it at all,

> But we putting our backs to the wall,
> To show the world we not festering
> Grenada has plans, yes, for improving.

The vital social function of calypso was reasserting itself and pulling itself away from the circumscription of smut, superficiality and anti-woman decadence, into which much of it had strayed under the dictatorship—even though there were always Grenadian calypsonians, like those of the We Tent, whose songs exposed the oppression they saw around them. Then after the Revolution, as the mass organizations grew in strength, confidence and membership and developed the new culture as one of their priorities, they threw up their own calypsonians—men and women who saw their prime function as using their art to defend the Revolution. In the fishing town of Gouyave, a group of Militia comrades came together to form their own musical combo. Valdon Boldeau, a young poet and calypsonian, explained the process:

Myself and another comrade, George Peters, are both members of the Gouyave Militia, and we were both writing poems and songs. Then there was an appeal that the Militia should be involved in other activities like sport, culture and community work. So on that basis we formed a cultural arm within our group and we found that many talented comrades in the Militia came forward. George wrote 'Destabilizers' and we sang it as a group, to warn those elements who are spreading lying propaganda against the Revolution and who are not involved in any positive work. It became very popular and was always being requested on Radio Free Grenada:[55]

DESTABILIZERS

They're stirring up all kind of strife
Trying to make men lose their life,
And we ent tell them
How to run their own affairs
Of their government,
But they're so fresh to tell we, just what we need
And what friends to keep,
But they never want to realize
Is we are the ones who fighting to survive!

CHORUS: *We ent want no fight*
We ent want no war,
Just leave we alone
Let we be we own —
But if they continue to destabilize,
Tell them is fire, fire, fire!

So many times we tried to strive
But obstacles just seemed to rise,
For many years we had to
Scrunt for a meal
And place to live,
Well, where were they to help we, in days of need
No one took heed,
But now as we country start to strive,
Every Tom, Dick and Harry come to rule we life.

They get uptight 'cause we unite,
They want to stir us up to fight,
Those imperialist puppets
Want to see us fall
Back to the dust,
But we are strong and nohow, they could keep us down
Down on the ground,
And though some of us may die,
Grenada will rise no matter what they try.

Some news media in the area
Find great pleasure in propaganda,
They always spreading all sorts
Of bad rumours
About Grenada,
But when it comes to speaking about the truth,
They wear a mute,
But we are a united *one*,
A model to the rest of the Caribbean.

George Peters, under his calypso name *Mighty Survivor*, went into the 1982 Carnival with another discerning calypso, exposing Reagan's Caribbean Basin Plan with a surging musical and lyrical energy:

CARIBBEAN BASIN PLAN FOR DOMINATION

Like these days just like days of plunder
The US forces will deploy all over,
But we condemn the Basin violation
By US forces in the Caribbean —
We know that they feel that they big and they heavy
And they could chop up everybody,
But that still can't shake we,
We prepared to fight for we country
We ent fraid of no Yankee —
Even though we faced with adverse condition
The fighting people of the Caribbean will stand!

CHORUS: *No, we say*
No, imperialism you must go
Get your filthy hands off we
We don't want your blood money.
The Caribbean Basin Plan
A demonstration of their kind
Exploitation in their hand
Bully who condemn their plan.

USA had their revolution
Thirteen years later they had their election,
And yet they vex we ent hold election
In only three years of Revolution —
But that is not why they really hate we,
They fraid the Caribbean follow we!
So they come right in the Caribbean
With their big Basin Plan
Trying to fool the Caribbean
With their three hundred million —
Like them Yankees really cannot understand,
They need to get some of we CPE Programme!

Let's refer to those days of plunder
When them pirates just rob all over,
Thief everything for the Queen of England
And she knight them for all they do wrong —
Like Columbus and Morgan the Pirate,
Sir Jack Hawkins and Lord Rodney!

Man they thief most of the Caribbean
Colonize it for England
Today we see US plunder
In the Caribbean area,
We know them Yankees want to start a war down here,
But the masses of this nation are prepared.

How can we fall for US 'ganda
When they support racist South Africa,
Support the fascist government in Chile,
El Salvador they sending military?
We don't forget how they bomb up Vietnam
Military aggressions and invasion —
And then they gone Argentina
Posing like big peacemaker
But then they have their dagger
Ready to stab Argentina —
Imperialism you empire falling down,
But the people's Revolution standing firm.

When Valdon Boldeau explains that, 'there has been a real growth in culture since the Revolution. It has brought forward a lot of expression that people were afraid to come out with before. The creative side of our people is now explode! All the feelings that were suppressed in Gairy days are exploding out!', the truth can be seen in the huge cultural output of such a small population. Culture has become synonymous with resistance, with fighting back, with defending the Revolution. Those themes have become a natural, inbuilt reaction against slander and misrepresentation. 'Senator' tells a story about when he was in Barbados as a part of the Grenada Carifesta delegation of 1981, which typifies the cultural response against attacks on the Revolution:

We were being confronted by some Barbadians as to what our process was here in Grenada. They had been subject to the worst media lies and were telling *us* what they thought was happening here. They were telling us all kinds of things about our *own* country, and we were getting quite angry at this kind of stupidness. When one man in partiuclar came out with some ridiculous things, I just found myself chanting to him automatically, without even thinking:

> Stop the propaganda
> Against Grenada
> Stop the propaganda
> Against Grenada . . .

and that chant later grew into a poem.[56]

The Militia

From the first seconds of the Grenada Revolution on the early morning of 13 March 1979, the Militia was born in action. Men and women seized guns from gairy's Green Beast army and police, and began to guard the beaches and patrol the roads. Songs were written and recorded which caught the reality of the people's determination to organize a serious volunteer defence force to withstand any attack from Gairy-bankrolled mercenaries or counter-revolutionaries:

> Stand firm! Patriot stand firm!
> Stand firm! Patriot stand firm!
> I love my country and so do you —
> Stand firm! Don't let the mercenary through.

National defence became one of the three main pillars of the Revolution, along with People's Democracy and the transformation of the economy. In Bernard Coard's words:

A Revolution which has the support of the people but which cannot defend itself very soon would be no revolution at all. Therefore the question of National Defence is another pillar without which there can be no revolution. Having the people but not having the material means for the people to defend themselves is a lesson we have to learn from Chile, Jamaica and other countries. But having the material means and not having the people is what Pinochet and Duvalier are all about. Therefore comrades, the people and the material means to defend the people are indispensable and interconnected in the process of the Revolution. That is why the question of the arming of all our people, the involvement of all our people in the People's Militia, is of such fundamental importance. The very process of building the Revolution creates the backlash, creates an impetus towards counter-revolution on the part of the enemies of all revolutions, on the part of imperialism. So, the second pillar is National Defence and the total involvement of all the people in National Defence.[57]

The Militia remains the strongest proof of the democratic involvement of the Grenadian people in their Revolution. The US State Department has already declared its belief that in relation to the size of its population, admittedly very small, Grenada has more people capable of using arms than any other country in the region. And this involves an entirely *voluntary* commitment, a fact which has caused Minister of National Mobilization, Selwyn Strachan, to describe the Militia as 'our most *formidable* democratic achievement':

> For here our people have answered the provocations of imperialism and organized themselves with the utmost seriousness and resolution for the most important task of all in our present phase — National Defence. You will find unemployed youths and grandmothers, small farmers and bankworkers, school students and teachers all ready, all vigilant all organized, all training side by side to defend their homeland. This *voluntary* people's militia, where our people are picking up guns every week to prepare to defend the benefits brought to them by *people's revolutionary democracy*, shows their ultimate commitment towards our process. For this same democracy, comrades, such as we are at the genesis of creating here in Grenada, is the greatest threat to the bogus, artificial and hypocritical lie of democracy that imperialism suspends over the world to cover up the repulsion and shame of its bloodsoaked crimes.[58]

Grenadian women have undoubtedly found their place in the Militia and play a leading role. 'Equal in Production and Defence' is becoming a reality in Grenada, and the Militia has become one of the most important catalysts in effecting this. In *Is Freedom We Making*, Dorcas Braveboy described the initial effect of the Militia training on many of her sisters, and how their attitudes gradually changed:

> Then I became involved in the Militia. It was clear that if we wanted the Revolution to succeed, then we had to be prepared to defend it. So I started training in my unit, and tried to persuade the other sisters to join in. Many of them said they didn't want to fire a gun, and so went into the service or medical sections. But when they got accustomed to gunfire, they started joining the infantry too.

This active involvement in defence of the Revolution by women in Grenada found its expression in the words of a young teacher from St David's Parish, Helena Joseph, who made her poem famous around the country by frequent public readings, which culminated at a rally after the Julien Fedon Manoeuvre in March 1981, where it received a massive ovation from her comrade Militia members:

I MILITIA

I Militia
I conscious militia
You Mr Exploiter
No way brother
Keeping down the worker
Saving your dollar
Making you richer
Ah say, is them labour
Not you sir

You spread propaganda
About Grenada
Through the media
And newspaper
Saying how we doh ha
Human rights in Grenada
And how we mustn't frien with Cuba
Asking them passenger
When they coming to Grenada
'Where you going to, Grenada?
Don't go over there
Is guns cover the whole area!'
And how Grenada is a disaster
How we have a big boat load ah dead soldier
Stinking in the harbour
Just come out and fight war in Nicaragua
And how they owe La Qua so much a dollar
But you must tell the truth sir
You dirty liar
Did you tell them that benefits has come
To all man and their brother in Grenada?
No, you din tell them that, aha
But I Militia is a conscious fighter

But you doh know sir
That the gun is we defender
And we had a manoeuvre
Which we say will never over
But let me tell you further too, Mr Exploiter
That I Militia will never be a supporter
Of your exploiting bourgeois, vampire behaviour
Why? Because I Militia ah conscious Militia

I Militia say
You can't live forever
You days getting fewer
Every minute, every hour
You blood sucker
Killing we nature

I Militia
I conscious Militia, say
You can't leave us to suffer
Is the heavy roller for you, Mr Exploiter
Ah pick up me AK, oppressor
To fight you counter
To free the worker
To build Grenada
I Militia will never surrender!

The nationwide manoeuvres themselves that have been held in Grenada by the People's Revolutionary Army and the Militia combined, as a response to US provocations and a part of the national defence training programme, have succeeded in binding the people together in a greater and greater sense of patriotic love and commitment to defend the benefits which the Revolution has brought them. The three-day Heroes of the Homeland Manoeuvre which followed closely in the wake of the Vieques provocations, and the Julien Fedon Manoeuvre which preceded the 13 March celebrations of 1982, both built up an extraordinary sense of unity amongst the population that was squarely behind the Revolution, as if the people all over the country were clenching themselves into one great fist. As Lieutenant-Colonel Ewart 'Headache' Layne of the People's Revolutionary Army said at the time of the Julien Fedon Manoeuvre:

Unlike last August, when they were coming out boldly and aggressively stating their intentions to invade the country, they have now recognized such boldness had the effect of galvanizing our people's unity and determination to stand up to them. Their tactic now is pretending to be quiet, for us to become complacent and less vigilant — but we shall never mix up the calm before the storm with the storm itself.

The imperialists are keeping quiet merely to fool us. Just as Fedon fought bravely against the British in 1795, defeating them time and time again, we in the same spirit would fight any aggressor, regardless of how strong and mighty the enemy may be, for just like Fedon we would never surrender![59]

The Militia members themselves share absolutely the determination of the regular army. Twenty-year-old Ray Redhead from Perdmontemps, St David's, after completing one of his unit's regular route marches, declared: 'For me and my country the Militia's most important in these times. The route march is a real mobilization for itself. As for manoeuvres, they play a vital part in keeping the soldiers fit and prepared. I was in the Militia from the time it started and I would like to urge all the youths to join it.'

In other statements from rank and file Militia members, published in *The Free West Indian*, their attitudes and resolution have also been crystal clear:

Being a militiaman is of extreme importance in this critical time. When you look at the world situation you see imperialism is in turmoil. It's falling gradually and almost getting outdated. The imperialists realize they are getting licks, so they are getting desperate.

A powerful militia and army is really needed here. Without it, we are not ready yet.

Eric Gittens, Belmont

There should be more training sessions for the Militia, and everyone should be taught to use more weapons defensively. I am prepared at any time to fight imperialism, to defeat them at all costs, regardless of the consequences.

Yvonne Duncan, Vincennes

I see defence as a priority in these times. When man sit down and analyze the Revolution, man could see the benefits coming to the people. That's the reason why I joined the People's Militia, because I want to contribute.

The second reason is when I see the threats at these times, especially of invasion.

It's true I like the Militia, because I realize that we as a people, have to train together to unite as one in combat. If we don't train together, we won't be able to fight together. I am calling on all not to wait till the time reach — learn to fight together now, because it could be in the next few hours, days, weeks, months, the invasion will come.

Wilby Stuart, St Paul's

In view of the threat faced by the country from external forces and local counters too, I felt it necessary as a patriot to contribute to the defence of my homeland. To me it is part of everyday life, you have to live with it.

Having been trained, I feel comfortable and know I am able to play a role in defence alongside the standing army. People should think twice about the reality of the situation in light of the present threat of US imperialism and other sources. For, in the case of an invasion, the reality is there will not be a few involved, it will be the country as a whole. I think everybody should see it as part of their business to defend the country and Revolution.

Basil Hypolite, St George's

To assist in defending the country I joined the Militia. Well, I gained a lot of experience being in it, and I feel it is something real good. I would like to encourage all who are not in the Militia to try to join immediately, for the whole of Grenada should be involved in military life. We should do so to save our lives.

Reila Christopher, Birchgrove

I joined the Militia most importantly because imperialism is intensifying its threat against the Revolution and I really saw the need to pick up a gun. I greatly enjoy being in the Militia and I always make it a priority, whether it's morning, evening, noon or night. I enjoy my training just as when I sit down to eat.

Make haste and join the Militia quick. It's those who are not in the Militia who will be hurt the most when the invasion comes. For they will not know what to do, when to do it and how to do it. I am confident our armed people will be able to beat back imperialism when they come.

Evril Sanderson, Lowther's Lane

The Revolution is threatened and it is all Grenadians' duty to defend it. If the Revolution fails, all Grenadians fail.

I love the Militia very much. It has become a part of my life, and being in the Militia is very necessary. Join the Militia today, get involved in the defence of your country and always remember, Grenada does not belong to the United States of America.

Larry Griffith, Woodlands

I joined the Militia to defend my country, my family and myself. I like the Militia because it is a means of defending the benefits gained by the Revolution.

All people who are not involved in the Militia should join right now, because your country needs you, your children needs you and your Revolution needs you.

Zinna Harford, Grand Mal[60]

The national journals themselves play an important mobilizing role in informing the people about the necessity of National Defence, and this is the absolute antithesis, of course, of the part played by the organs of the enemies of the people's cause in Guyana, Chile and Jamaica — and that of *The Torchlight* too, which treacherously exposed to Grenada's enemies the exact locations of her main defence installations. In 'Militia Corner', which was a regular feature of *The Free West Indian* during 1981, the lessons of Jamaica in particular were driven home time and time again. Under a headline, 'It's a struggle to preserve the peace', the writer quoted a Militia statement:

In Jamaica, for example, reactionary forces in and out of the country, aided by the powerful reactionary media, consistently attacked the progressive Michael Manley government for spending too much time, energy and resources on Jamaica's defence, while at the same time, with imperialism's aid, they were accelerating their opposition until the government was overthrown.

Grenadians cherish peace, but peace can only be guaranteed by the people's ability to defend their revolutionary democratic process, and as such, all Grenadian patriots have a role to play in preserving peace in their country.[61]

The Militia brings old and young together and breaks down all artificial barriers caused by age, sex, race or religion. As Philbert Thomas, a sixty-one-year-old Public Works road cleaner from Sauteurs said in *Is Freedom We Making*:

> I goes to the Militia every Wednesday night. You see, I'd do anything for the Revo. We learn a lot at the Militia; how the older must respect the younger, and how the younger must know how to behave themself. We is all together as one people. We drill and we train together, young and old. I never hold a gun before, but if Gairy or the mercenaries come, we go bury them in the sea, they never be able to make it.

Militia groups exist in each village, and are fast becoming catalysts of culture and sport, as well as military training. During August 1982, for example, Region One Group held 'combat relay races' from St David's to St George's Market Square with competitors dressed in full combat gear, and carrying 120 rounds of ammunition. As in every institution of the Grenada Revolution, continuous review, self-criticism and criticism and democratic involvement of the members through general meetings, the creation of workplans and sessions of analysis are an integral part of being a Militia member. For democracy is its driving force, as it is the dynamo behind every aspect of the Grenada Revolution. For ultimately, it is not only the *form* the Revolution takes, but the participation and involvement that it brings, that also provides the content and rationale for why the Grenadian people are united as one to beat back the many-headed monster of imperialist destabilization:

> For when we ask of our people to step forward to defend the gains and benefits of their Revolution, we are using no pressure, no compulsion. We are saying in effect: 'This is your Revolution, it is your democratic right to defend it.' For as we know, democracy brings responsibilities and rights in equal measure, and our people, in their huge and patriotic response to join our People's Revolutionary Militia and in their understanding of the full impact of our slogan, *The manoeuvre will never over!*, are clearly realizing this. They are making the profound and proud choice of a free people; to hold fast to what is theirs, and it is theirs because they are *involved*, brain and muscle, action and speech, in the building of a new, vibrant and loving Grenada.
>
> *Maurice Bishop*, New Year Address, 1 January 1982

Notes and References

Part 1: From Crown Colony to People's Revolution

1. Quoted in W Richard and Ian Jacobs: *Grenada: the route to revolution*, (1980)
2. Interview with Agatha Francis by CS, from *To Construct from Morning: making the People's Budget in Grenada*, (1982)
3. Quoted in *In the Spirit of Butler: trade unionism in free Grenada*, (1982)
4. From E M Gairy's address at the opening of the Third Easter Water Parade, 26 March, 1978
5. From E M Gairy's address at the opening of the Second Easter Water Parade, 8 April 1977
6. Pamphlet published by Government Printery (1972)
7. From State Broadcast by E M Gairy, 27 April 1973
8. From State Broadcast by E M Gairy, 30 April 1971
9. From State Broadcast by E M Gairy, 27 April 1973
10. ibid
11. From *Manifesto of the New Jewel Movement*, November 1973
12. From 'Crisis '74', a collective poem by trainee teachers Stephen Andrew, Donald Barrett, Denzil Modest, Clarice Frederick, Rena Charles, Anasthasia Francis, Rudolph Logan, Myrna Hagley
13. From song 'Bloody Sunday', Mamma Cannes Group, St David's, Grenada, 1981
14. From Interview with Selwyn Strachan, *The Free West Indian*, 17 November 1982
15. From interview with Mrs Alimenta Bishop by CS, June 1982
16. See interview with Sydney John in *In the Spirit of Butler*
17. From interview with Phyllis Coard by CS, June 1982
18. From interview with Edwin Frank by CS, June 1982
19. From interview with Emelda Telesford by CS from introduction of *Carriacou and Petit Martinique: in the mainstream of the revolution* (1982)
20. Interview with garment worker Doreen Lewis by CS from *To Construct from Morning*
21. From song 'Freedom Day' by Cecil 'Flying Turkey' Belfon, St George's, 1981

Part 2: Come the Revolution, Come Destabilization

22. *The Free West Indian*, 6 June 1981
23. *The Free West Indian*, 22 August 1981
24. *Caribbean Contact*, September, 1981
25. *The Free West Indian*, 21 November 1981

26.   *The Free West Indian*, 22 November 1980
27.   Interview with Sydney 'Godzilla' John: *In the Spirit of Butler*
28.   *The Free West Indian*, July 1981
29.   *Workers' Voice*, October 1981
30.   'Grenada's Revolution: An Interview with Bernard Coard':
      Race and Class XXI, (1979) and reproduced in pamphlet form as
      Grenada: let those who labour hold the reins (1980)
31.   *The Free West Indian*, 28 March 1981
32.   *The Free West Indian*, 27 June 1971
33.   *The New Jewel*, 28 May 1982
34.   Supplement. *The Free West Indian*, March 1982
35.   *The New Jewel*, April 1981
36.   Interview with Comrade Bernard Coard by Don Rojas and CS:
      To Construct from Morning
37.   *The Free West Indian*, 15 August 1981
38.   *The Free West Indian*, 4 March 1981
39.   The full text of this speech appears in *In the Spirit of Butler*.
40.   *Caribbean Contact*, September, 1981
41.   *The Free West Indian*, 12 September 1981

Part 3: No Backward Reaction could Stop our Revolution!

42.   From speech by Comrade Bishop: 'Organize to Fight Destabil-
      ization, 8 May 1979
43.   From *Tongues of the New Dawn:* an anthology of poems (1982)
44.   From literacy manual, *Let Us Learn Together*, (Centre for
      Popular Education, St George's, 1980)
45.   From *Adult Literacy: Book 1* (Centre for Popular Education, St
      George's, 1982)
46.   From Comrade Bishop's speech at the Opening of the National
      In-service Teacher Education Programme, 30 October 1980.
      Quoted in full in *Grenada: Education is a Must!* (1981)
47.   From *Tongues of the New Dawn*
48.   *The Free West Indian*, 13 September 1980
49.   *The Free West Indian*, 18 April 1981
50.   See chapter 1 of *Is Freedom We Making* by Merle Hodge and
      Chris Searle
51.   From interview with Frederick Grant. *In the Spirit of Butler*
52.   Ligarou — vampire
53.   *Maccoo* — a stupid person, blockhead
54.   Bernadette, Laurice, Laureen: the Christian names of the three
      young women killed in the 19 March 1980 bombing in Queen's
      Park: Alister Strachan, killed by Gairy's police on 19 June 1977;
      Rupert Bishop, killed by Gairy's police on 21 January 1974
55.   From interview with Valdon Boldeau by CS, July 1982
56.   From interview with Michael Mitchell by CS, May 1982

57. From 'National Reconstruction and Development in the Grenadian Revolutionary Process': Speech by Comrade Coard at the First Conference in Solidarity with the Grenada Revolution. Published in *Grenada is not Alone* (1982)

58. From 'Mass Participation in the Democratic Process': Speech by Comrade Strachan at the First Conference in Solidarity with the Grenada Revolution. Published in *Grenada is not Alone*

59. *The Free West Indian*, 5 February 1982

60. *The Free West Indian*, 19 September 1981; 1 May 1982

61. *The Free West Indian*, March 1981

BIBLIOGRAPHY

The Grenada Revolution

BAIN, Francis J, *Beyond the Ballot Box: a brief enquiry into the Grenada Revolution*, Grenada Publishers, St George's, 1980

BISHOP, Maurice, and SEARLE, Chris, *Grenada: Education is a Must!* Britain/Grenada Friendship Society, London, 1981

COARD, Bernard, (interviewed by Chris Searle), *Grenada: let those who labour hold the reins*, Liberation, London, 1981

DABREO, D. Sinclair, *The Grenada Revolution*, MAPS, St Lucia, 1979

EPICA Task Force, *Grenada: the peaceful revolution*, Epica, Washington, 1982

HODGE, Merle, and SEARLE, Chris, *Is Freedom We Making: the new democracy in Grenada*, Government Information Service, St George's 1981

HOLNESS, Chris, 'The Political Situation in Grenada', *Socialism* Vol II No 1, January 1975

JACOBS, W Richard, and Ian, *Grenada: the route to revolution*, Casa de las Americas, Havana, 1979

LUNA, Jorge, *Grenada: la nueva joya del Caribe*, Editorial de Ciencias Sociales, Havana, 1982

MANUEL, Sam, and PULLEY, Andrew, *Grenada: revolution in the Caribbean*, Pathfinder, New York, 1982

SEARLE, Chris, (editor), *Carriacou and Petite Martinique: in the mainstream of the revolution*, Fedon Publishers, St George's, 1982

Other Works

Collected Speeches of Maurice Bishop, Casa de las Americas, Havana 1982

Freedom Has No Price: an anthology of poems, Festival of the Revolution, St George's, 1981

Grenada is not Alone, Fedon Publishers, St George's, 1981

In the Spirit of Butler: trade unionism in free Grenada, Fedon Publishers, St. George's 1981

To Construct from Morning: making the People's Budget in Grenada, Fedon Publishers, St. George's, 1982

Tongues of the New Dawn: an anthology of Poems, Festival of the Revolution, St. George's 1981

Forward Ever! The Speeches of Maurice Bishop: Pathfinder, Sydney, Australia, 1983

APPENDIX A

Interview with Maurice Bishop, Prime Minister of Grenada

SEARLE: *Why do you think that imperialism is so obsessively afraid of the Grenada Revolution, an obsession out of all proportion to the size of the country?*

BISHOP: There are several reasons for this. The first is the fact that Grenada was the first country in the English-speaking Caribbean to have had a successful revolution, and different US administrations have always shown a mortal fear of any revolutionary process, of any attempt by any people by revolutionary means to overthrow different dictatorships or oligarchies that are oppressing them. These administrations have, of course, conveniently forgotten the history of their own country and their own revolution in 1776.

The second reason is even more fundamental and relates to the gains, successes and achievements of the Grenada Revolution. The fact is that coming from a base that is no different and in many respects much worse than most other Caribbean territories of similar size and a similar type of economy, we have been able in three and a half years to reduce unemployment from the fantastically high figure of some 50 per cent of the total workforce — and among women 70 per cent — down to 14.7 per cent, which means a drop of over 35 per cent in the unemployment rate. And this at a time when other countries both inside and outside our region were continuing to have difficulties in finding jobs for their people, and this too as Grenada was being subjected to massive propaganda destabilization, economic aggression, military threat and diplomatic isolation.

Thirdly there is the question of health, and the fact that we have been able to bring free health care to our people, to more than double the numbers of our doctors, quintuple the number of our dentists and increased by seven times the number of dental clinics in our country. All of this again is something that the people of the region are watching very closely. And there is Education too. At this point in time, through the Centre for Popular education programme, illiteracy has been virtually wiped out in the country and is estimated now at being something like 3 per cent of the population. A massive adult education programme has also started as Phase Two of the Centre for Popular Education, and at the same time we have been able to increase dramatically the number of places for students going to secondary schools. Before the Revolution only 11 per cent of all the eligible students were able to get into the secondary schools: now that figure has been increased to 36 per cent and we hope within the next two to three years to move to universal secondary education. The availability of free university scholarships abroad is also a part of that process. Moving from a situation of three in the last year of Gairy, we increased that paltry figure within the first six months of the Revolution to one hundred and nine students being able to go abroad on free university scholarships. Then there is free secondary education which we have introduced for all secondary schools in the country, and there is also a programme of subsidized school uniforms and school books for the poorest children.

Over the past three years in our economy we have been able to achieve an accumulated growth rate of some 10 per cent. The World Bank, in its last report of August 1982, spoke in very glowing terms about the strides which we have been able to make in the economy, in terms of economic management, planning, fiscal and budgetary controls — really in terms of all aspects of the development of our economy. That again is something that has certainly not gone unnoticed by the people of the region. Another significant point to be made in relation to gains and benefits are the structures of revolutionary grassroots democracy that we are building in Grenada, away from the Westminster parliamentary system to a form which allows the people themselves to participate on a regular basis, at least once a month, through the system of mass organizations that have been built very rapidly, and the organs of popular power — the Zonal Councils, Workers' Parish Councils and the Farmer, Women and Youth Councils.

In the critical area of housing, too, the Revolution has realized many advances. The Housing Repair Programme has been a major achievement. In 1980 this programme saw the renovation of the homes of 593 families; the figure rose to 981 in 1981 and will be about 1,300 by the end of 1982, constituting an overall total of 2,874. The money spent amounted to 2,243,415 Eastern Caribbean dollars. We have to remember that in Grenada the average size of the family in the low income bracket for which the programme was designed is seven persons. Thus, the number of persons benefiting from the Housing Repair Programme is in fact 20,118 — a figure which represents nearly 20% of our population.

The Revolution has also witnessed the introduction of several housing schemes. These have been completed in Telescope and Grand Anse, while others are on a stream in Corinth, Grand Anse, Telescope and Waltham. Construction here will receive a tremendous boost with the new Sandino Plant which has the capacity of producing some five hundred houses per year.

Infrastructural development too has been a major achievement of our Revolution. The truth is that the face of Grenada is changing before our very eyes. By early 1984, we would have become the very first Caribbean country to have built an international airport after its independence — everyone else had theirs built during the colonial era. By the end of 1982, we would have built about fifty new miles of farm and feeder roads, which is an unprecedented rate of progress, and our new Eastern Main Road (being one of the three main roads in our country) should be nearly halfway completed. By August 1983 we should have direct dialling facilities to our sister islands of Carriacou and Petit Martinique for the first time in our history, and shortly after that we would have more than doubled the number of existing telephone lines in the country. Electricity output will go up by over 50 per cent in 1983 when we install our two recently purchased generators. We now deliver daily 50 per cent more pipe-borne water into the homes of our people than could have been done before the Revolution, and this process will be further enhanced in 1983 when construction of the new Mamma Cannes Reservoir in St David's is completed. Two new schools were built this year and at least one more will be constructed in 1983, while at the same time more community centres, day care and pre-primary facilities and health centres will continue to be rehabilitated and built throughout the course of next year.

So for reasons such as these concrete benefits, imperialism is doubly worried and concerned about our revolutionary process, because they fear that the new socio-economic and political path of development which we have embarked upon may prove to be an example to the rest of the region, and therefore the people of the region may begin to press their own governments for a similar process to start in their own countries. Additionally, there is the fact that since the Revolution, Grenada has pursued an independent and nonaligned path, and different US administrations over the years — but in particular this present administration of President Ronald Reagan — is deathly afraid of any independence, of nonaligned commitment in the world, particularly by countries of the Third World, which they feel they have a divine right to dominate and exploit. So when we take firm positions that we are entitled to legal equality, to mutual respect for sovereignty, to noninterference in our internal affairs, to ideological pluralism and the right to develop our own process free from all outside interference and *diktat*, obviously it is seen as a mortal insult to this American administration. Equally, when we decide that as a part of our policy of nonalignment, that we are entitled to diversify and develop our relations with countries of the world, particularly the socialist countries, then this is seen as adding insult to injury. So the fact is that this firm and fundamental position of maintaining an independent and nonaligned path of development, and a nonaligned position in our international relations, is one that has caused us real problems with his American administration.

Finally, we have gleaned from their own security reports which they have put out — not publicly, but which we have nevertheless seen — other insights. In one of these reports the particular point was made that Grenada's process has two big differences to the other two revolutionary processes in the region, in Cuba and Nicaragua. For on the one hand, we speak the same language — English — as the people of the USA, and on the other hand we have a largely black population. What they have pointed out from this is that the Grenada Revolution therefore has a facility of speaking directly to, and appealing directly in their own language to the people of the USA overall, but more so to the exploited majority. Then in the case of black Americans, meaning something like twenty seven million black people who are a part of the most rejected and oppressed section of the American population, US imperialism has a particular dread that they will develop an extra empathy and rapport with the Grenada Revolution, and from that point of view will pose a threat to their own continuing control and domination of the blacks inside the US.

SEARLE: *How did your experience of fascist terror under the Gairy régime serve as an efficient apprenticeship to organizing against imperialist destabilization since the Revolution?*

BISHOP: What we learned from our experiences in the struggle against the dictator has proved to be very critical in many respects. Firstly, of course, it deepened our organizational skill and ability and gave us a tremendous experience in fighting in underground situations. We had to produce our newspaper, for example, in clandestine conditions, which meant that every single week we had to go to some new venue in order to print it, and thereafter our network of distributors had to sell the newspaper without being caught by the Gairy repressive apparatus. This was the invaluable kind of organizational ability we had to develop from underground in the building of our party. We had to hold our meetings while the dictatorship was searching for us, and this served to force us to develop a strong sense of security and to build firm alliances with the people of our country coming from many different classes and strata. Very often we had to hold meetings in houses that would be unlikely to attract attention. That whole experience certainly helped us in our subsequent policy of building a concrete alliance to fight the 1976 elections, and it continues to help us today in pursuing a policy of alliances with sections of the upper petite-bourgeoisie in our country, and even the bourgeoisie, as part of our overall policy of socialist orientation.

It also helped to steel our comrades, helped to make them much, much more disciplined, helped to ensure that once they were given tasks then they would carry them out, because in situations that we faced it was absolutely critical to be dead certain that everybody was actually doing what he or she had promised to do. And this was linked to the necessity of collective leadership. We found from our very hard experience that the repression was so constant and consistent, that at any given time any number of our people might be arrested or charged or jailed, or sometimes, and this happened quite frequently, beaten, and therefore unavailable. So this made it necessary for us to build a strong collective leadership and rely very much upon each other, ensuring that each of us was responsible for specific critical tasks and areas. That also has stood us in very good stead in terms of ensuring that our principle of collective leadership that we still follow, is fully maintained.

That period certainly helped us in making us much firmer. That quality of firmness has come out of the repression, out of the need repeatedly to show courage in the face of numerous difficulties, of having to come back from behind after temporary setbacks which we never accepted as defeats, and which also forced us to see things always in strategic terms and not just in tactical terms. We were always very certain that, no matter how many individual skirmishes Gairy and his forces might win, eventually our revolutionary forces would triumph.

Those years of fighting against the dictatorship also made us very aware of the international situation. Gairy's closest links and friendships were with dictatorships and fascist regimes in Chile, in South Korea and Haiti. Seeing these alliances at work, and seeing also in the context of the Caribbean those reactionary régimes out here who gave him support — some of whom now are precisely the ones that are most opposed to our Revolution — really helped to teach us a lot about the international situation, about who our friends and enemies really were, and what we have subsequently seen as being the pillars of our foreign policy.

But most crucially, the experiences of combating the Gairy dictatorship taught us the fundamental importance of having the firmest and most constant contacts with the people, working with the masses at all times, being totally honest with them at all times, in periods when we had to hide and in periods of relative lull, whether it was for the mass mobilization activity which we did so well before the Revolution and which we have continued to stress since the Revolution, or whether it was creating democratic structures and the embryonic youth and women's organizations which have flourished so prosperously since our grasp of power on 13 March 1979. We have learned to develop a truly deep and abiding respect for the people of our country, particularly the working people, and have understood more and more their enormous creative power and ability to confront and solve all their problems.

SEARLE: *What precedents and new techniques has imperialism devised in its strategy of trying to destabilize the Grenada Revolution?*

BISHOP: In this present phase, imperialism has created a number of new strategies which themselves are different from its onslaughts over the last twenty-five years upon Guyana, Chile and Jamaica. Our Revolution has clearly forced imperialist destabilization to find new approaches and become more and more wickedly original in its counter-revolutionary techniques. In Grenada there is no US Embassy, and this has clearly placed a powerful brake upon their potential to destabilize the Revolution internally, not having the permanent base for their mischief which they had in the three other countries mentioned. The US imperialists and their CIA are thus forced to rely upon local agents which they first have to recruit internally then contact clandestinely from time to time, but in Grenada they do not have this fixed facility and infrastructure to operate, they do not have this ready-made system. The guise of normal diplomatic relations — which only hid on-the-spot organizational and recruitment centres — enabled them to reach their agents and gain information on a daily basis, as well as to provide guidance to those unpatriotic elements within the country who were prepared to carry out the dirty work of the CIA. This is a critical disadvantage for them in relation to Grenada.

Then our dismantling of the Westminster parliamentary system is also important in this context. Along with that dismantling has come an end to the traditional tribalism which continues in other Caribbean countries. A part of that political tribalism, as used by the CIA, has been to get some of the parliamentarians to use the medium of parliament in such a way as to destabilize the country. Masterminded by their American puppeteers, they raise bogus concerns about the economy, they spread vicious propaganda from outside the country and seek to make the people lose faith and confidence in their revolutionary government, raising a million and one other such provocative matters through the medium of parliament — and thus claim to do it in that sense with a certain measure of legitimacy.

In relation to the media, we made it very clear at an early stage that we were not prepared to countenance counter-revolutionary literature in our country, or media that were being used for the purpose of inciting sections of the population to violence or disaffection. So within the first six months of the Revolution, one counter-revolutionary newspaper, *The Torchlight*, was closed down, and that too has meant that a powerful arm of their destabilization machinery has been amputated in our situation.

Then there is the question of the armed forces, which in the Chile and Jamaica situations, for example, remained intact after progressive governments had taken power. For us it was very different. In the first hours of the Revolution the Green Beast army of Gairy was completely disbanded. That meant that thereafter a new army came into being, an army of patriotic youth, young farmers and sections of the unemployed. Right from the start it was possible to imbue this young army with a patriotic, anti-imperialist consciousness, and that has proved to be a decisive factor. The possibilities of infiltration or of *coups d'état* are much more difficult in this army than in those countries where the armed forces of the previous régime remained intact. On top of that we have built a people's militia in addition to our regular armed forces, something that did not happen in the three countries that were mentioned before, where the progressive régimes did not move to arm the people in that way. The value of the people's militia is that the whole question of defence becomes the responsibility not just of a standing, full-time, professional army, but also of the whole people, who are ready to face any threat.

Within three years we have made greater attempts to disentangle our economy from the clutches of imperialism. The Marketing and National Importing Board which we established now has removed the opportunity for unpatriotic elements of the bourgeoisie to create artificial shortages of essential foods and supplies, a factor which was very prevalent in Jamaica in particular during the last years of the Manley Government. Furthermore we have attempted to involve our people in the planning and running of the economy, to get them to understand that the question of economic construction is not just an issue for the government, but is also the responsibility of the people. Therefore there has been a great deal more voluntary involvement in the building of the economy in our situation than perhaps there was in either Chile or Jamaica. That too has been a major factor in terms of the room imperialism would have to manouevre in our situation.

Inside our country there are no media which they can use, so they have moved very powerfully into the regional media, the newspapers and the dozens of radio stations of the region daily beaming into our country, trying to spread lies and distortions about the Revolution. This has been a dramatic and unprecedented factor of huge intensity that we have had constantly to confront. We have seen the spectacle of five of these regional newspapers — the Jamaica *Gleaner,* the *Advocate* and *Nation* from Barbados and the *Express* and *Guardian* from Trinidad — coming out, as they did in November 1981, with the same headlines, the same front-page editorial attacking the Revolution and calling for our isolation. Again, this month, exactly one year later, we have seen almost an exact repetition, this time on the occasion of our presence at the CARICOM Heads of Government Conference in Jamaica, when all five newspapers carried the same back-page paid advertisement, prompted by its publication in *The Gleaner* on the first day of the Conference — another vulgar attack which had the effect of completely exposing who really runs the media in the region and what the so-called independent 'Free Press' really means. We saw again the same small minority tied to corporate interests speaking each time for their class and never for the interests, concerns and issues facing the masses of working people in the region. In fact, following the classic front-page fiasco of November 1981, journalists in the region, most notably the Trinidad and Tobago journalists, came out totally condemning the actions of their newspaper bosses, with one editor declaring that he had no idea that co-ordinated attacks on Grenada such as his newspaper had been party to, were being waged right through the region, with newspapers such as the one he himself edited! This only showed once again who were the real controllers, the real bosses, the real dragons of big business.

This extraordinary level of co-ordinated vulgarity, not even known in the Western European or American press, is highly significant, and says a lot about the deep penetration of imperialism into the regional press to force it to carry out its masters' dirty orders. Recently again the same newspapers all carried an article which alleged that in ten crates our government had received 'Russian Migs'. All of the forces behind these newspapers know well that Grenada does not have the capacity to operate 'Migs', in terms of what would be required in the way of hangars, maintenance facilities, trained pilots and technicians — it is a physical impossibility in Grenada, and all of them know that. They know, too, that if such planes came into our country, it could not be done secretly. Of course, the very way in which these articles were written exposed that they knew all that. One article declared that one of our government officials had been contacted and had said that the story was impossible and must be a journalistic joke. But then the writer of the article continued: 'But in any case, *if it is true*, then it shows how dangerous this Grenada Government is etc. etc.', and went on to spend the rest of the page attacking us with a whole pile of lies. So it is quite clear that this was yet one more attempt at propaganda destabilization, but this time using a higher and clearer form, because they were discovering that their lies about the economy or human rights violations did not convince the Caribbean masses, so now they try another grotesque tack to try to make us appear as if we are a military threat to our neighbours.

Another precedent set in the methodology of destabilization was shown to us by the United States International Communications Agency (USICA) in May 1981. This propaganda limb of the US State Department summoned all the editors of the various Caribbean newspapers to Washington and showed them the best they could offer in facilities in the media and press, then held a number of seminars and workshops with them. One of the things that emerged was that an offer was made to these editors of assistance to develop their own facilities, but that it would only be forthcoming if they collaborated in helping to isolate Grenada through adverse propaganda. And sure enough, within a very short time from the return of these editors, a massive propaganda campaign started against us from their pages in the region. So the USICA Conference type of approach was certainly one new and creative destabilization strategy developed by US imperialism to try to bring down our Revolution.

Then we have recently discovered yet another destabilization phenomenon. Just prior to any major conference in the region that we go to, or any significant event in our own country, they will try to get reactionary trade union leaders or other individuals and backward institutions in the region to host conferences, sometimes conferences ostensibly dealing with conventional areas, maybe just normal trade union questions or questions of so-called democracy or human rights as interpreted by them. But these conferences will be set in the particular countries we are about to go to a few days before we are due to arrive. So that when we recently went off to Organization of Eastern Caribbean States for a Heads of Government conference in St Lucia, we found that the week before a number of these reactionary trade union leaders were in St Lucia holding a conference. This conference was apparently dealing with regular worker issues like national insurance schemes, but what additionally happened was that a well-known Grenadian counter-revolutionary exile called Stanley Cyrus, plus a Cuban counter-revolutionary exile, arrived at the conference and steered it into vulgar attacks against Grenada in particular, but also Cuba and Nicaragua. A number of documents were also distributed, obviously preparing the ground for when we arrived a few days later. Then something very similar happened in Jamaica a few days before we landed for the CARICOM Heads of Government meeting, when another conference was focussing upon issues like democracy and elections — and that was precisely one of the issues, Westminster Parliamentary Democracy, that Tom Adams and Edward Seaga, Prime Ministers of Barbados and Jamaica respectively, were attempting to push at the CARICOM meeting, hoping to secure an amendment to the CARICOM Treaty to institutionalize the Westminster approach to the question of democracy.

SEARLE: *How has the Revolution managed continually to beat back destabilizing mischief, whilst other processes have failed?*

BISHOP: We have only done this through our relations of total honesty with our people. We start from the basis that destabilization can only really work when it is covered up, when it is operating under darkness. Thus from the earliest days of the Revolution, whenever we perceived any threat we always informed the people. The speech that I gave just one month after the Revolution, dealing with the threats made by US Ambassador Ortiz to us, was on national radio and television, and it exposed these threats to Grenada and the young Revolution to the people in the first few days. Then after three months there was another speech: 'Organize to Fight Destabilization', in which we exposed the CIA Pyramid Plan. Again, there was the national address given on the issue of the two Roman Catholic priests who were developing a whole strategy of destabilization, and that again was a national address, when we dealt fully with the issues raised. Or there was the way in which we handled the 'Gang of Twenty-six', who published the so-called *Grenadian Voice* as a cover for their counter-revolutionary activity, and they also were totally exposed at the rally of 19 June 1981.

So our first line of defence is complete openness and honesty: tell our people all the facts and call upon them for a response and involve them in what is happening. Linked to that is the necessity of the maximum preparation we can have through the involvement of our people, and here the militia is crucial, ensuring that at the level of national defence the people are always there and are always ready and able to defend the process, the Revolution and the country. We believe that the Revolution can only develop around three pillars: first the people and their democratic organizations, secondly the building of a strong national economy, and thirdly the building of a national defence capacity. We try at all times to integrate these three pillars because we feel that if any one of the three is missing at any particular time, then the Revolution will be in danger and will be weakened.

But we can also speak of a fourth pillar, the pillar of international relations, and that too has been a major way of fighting destabilization. Whenever there is any threat to our process we immediately appeal to all our friends around the world for their support. This was very evident, for example, during the US 'Amber and the Amberines' manoeuvre, staged by the imperialist armed forces in August 1981 off the island of Vieques, near Puerto Rico. Our response was to go on a major international offensive around the issue and to call upon all friendly governments and international institutions, political parties and organizations we had contacts with, and ask them to come out with strong statements against the provocation which was a dress rehearsal for the invasion of our country. In the case of friendly governments, we asked them to summon the American ambassadors in their countries to demand explanations. That proved to be a very successful diplomatic offensive on our part, and we struggled in a similar way when we were having difficulties with the World Bank and the International Monetary Fund after we had made an application for the Supplementary Fund facility, and it was rejected at the last minute as a result of the veto by the American director on the Board of Directors. Again we went on a worldwide offensive and mobilized all our friends to come to our support and intervene on our behalf on that question.

We have also seen — and there is much evidence of this in the account that precedes — the Revolution laying great emphasis upon the cultural awareness and educational development of our people, through literacy programmes and rallies, mass events, councils and panel discussions, and through our growing and prospering organs of people's democracy, so that our people fully understand the extent of the imperialist penetration and the ways in which they can systematically and successfully fight against it.

APPENDIX B

Notes on Destabilization: an interview with Cheddi Jagan

SEARLE: *Could you help me define destabilization from your own experience of it, particularly in relationship to the struggle in Guyana?*

JAGAN: First of all, the word 'destabilization' came into currency after the 1973 coup in Chile which overthrew Allende's government. Kissinger was the first person who used it in this particular sense. This was after the CIA had said that they had no responsibility for the coup, but then, under pressure of a US Senate Investigating Committee Kissinger eventually admitted that the CIA was involved. The way it was done in Chile had been rehearsed in Guyana, but at that particular time in Guyana in the 1950s and 1960s there was not much awareness of what was going on.

The aim of imperialism is to prevent a revolutionary process, and wherever you have governments which want to make fundamental changes — to change economic structures and bring in new models of development which are people-oriented then imperialism will try to overthrow any such government.

There are various methods. Firstly there is the overt method where you have *direct intervention*. We had that in Guyana in 1953, when the Churchill Government sent warships and removed us, the People's Progressive Party, from government after we had been there for only four and a half months. Then there was a massive intervention in the Dominican Republic in 1965, and that was able to defeat the revolutionary forces that had already virtually captured the capital city.

However, with the kind of computer mentality that the ruling circles of America were acting with, they tried the same kind of thing more massively in Vietnam. But the computer didn't bargain for the different kind of situation that there was in Vietnam. There you had a communist party, with long experience in struggle, and that communist party had created a broad front which brought in the other popular parties, trade unions, other mass organizations, women's organizations, religious bodies and so on. Of course, due to this, the forces of US imperialism were defeated there. And since that defeat in this *direct* method, Nixon enunciated what is called a 'Vietnamization Policy'. That is, it is cheaper and less problematical for US internal politics — for the Vietnam War radicalized those too — to base a policy upon using American money to get Asians to fight Asians, then Africans must fight Africans and Latin Americans and the people of the Caribbean must also fight each other. It is cheaper that way for America and it doesn't create political problems *inside* the country.

This was a change in the form of destabilization where*proxies* were used. We saw this when the Americans withdrew from the Dominican Republic, and the Brazilian dictatorship moved in to maintain so-called 'Law and Order'. In other cases, troops from neighbouring countries were used to put down progressive rebellions — like in the Shaba Province of Mobutu's Zaire in 1977, Egypt sent troops, and so did Morocco, and the revolutionaries were dislodged. That is another example of the 'Vietnamization Model' that imperialism uses.

Then you have the *indirect aggression,* where the imperialists stay behind the scenes, but finance and prepare the whole thing. You had that in Guatemala in 1954, where reactionary exiles were trained in the jungles of Nicaragua and then they went into Guatemala and overthrew the progressive government of Arbenz. That is the same method which, having succeeded in Guatemala, was used against Cuba in 1961. The exiled Cubans, the Gusanos who were trained in Guatemala, invaded Cuba with CIA backing; but they failed miserably when they were defeated by the Cuban people at Playa Giron.

Other forces of destabilization use less overt means and work through gradual subversion. This method can take many forms — working through students, trade unions, setting up political parties, through churches and so on. And all those forces would work together to destabilize a revolutionary or democratic government. Anti-communism was a weapon used against

Cuba and us in Guyana when we formed the government, and now Grenada too is facing the same kind of anti-communist hysteria. The CIA once paid a million dollars to Norman Thomas, who headed the Socialist Party of America, and he admitted that he set up seventeen socialist parties through Latin America to fight communism. So that is fighting from the so-called left! There may be all kinds of splinter groups doing the same thing, being financed indirectly, or even directly, by the CIA to do disruptive work which can undermine the process.

Another agency is the Church. It was disclosed in 1967, when the CIA exposé first took place in *Ramparts* magazine, that the CIA had got under its control the National Students' Association, and they were getting one million dollars a year which they were using to help finance Billy Graham's Latin American Crusade. And in Guyana we knew that both before and after the 1961 elections the Anti-communist Crusade was operating. The head of the organization sent his lieutenant, a Dr Sluis, to Guyana and admitted also that he had asked for $100,000 but only received $48,000 for his trouble! If he had received the full amount he might have caused us to be defeated in 1961, as he would have been able to spread more lies and propaganda that there is no place for religion under communism, and thus cause a lot of confusion among the people.

We had another example when the American Embassy people actually went out on the streets with anti-Cuban and anti-Soviet films, identifying us with Cuba and the Soviet Union, and saying their would be no freedom in Guyana under the PPP. This was exposed by the 'Insight', team of the London *Sunday Times* in April, 1967 under the titles 'How the CIA got rid of Jagan' and 'Macmillan/Sandys back CIA plot'. These articles exposed how the CIA agents were working within the American Consulate in Georgetown.

Then we had the newspapers. In Guyana, one of the daily papers was owned by the leader of the anti-communist, anti-socialist, pro-catholic, pro-imperialist third party, the United Force. The Catholic Church, meanwhile, was working with the Anti-communist Christian Crusade and had created its own local organization: 'Defenders of Freedom'. The Press virtually incited the people against us. They began to spread the propaganda that the PPP was a 'coolie' government and what they called a 'rice government', because we were concentrating our development programme upon agriculture. We did this because the British would not allow us, in their overall policy towards their colonies, to have an industrial programme. Then the agreements that I had made with Cuba, Hungary and the German Democratic Republic — all of that was held up by the colonial office. For while I could sign a trade agreement, as I did with Cuba, under the constitution of internal self-government we couldn't sign an aid agreement, as 'aid' came under Foreign Affairs. So objectively, agricultural projects in the countryside, like irrigation and drainage schemes, were all that we were allowed to do! Now most of the black population, and in particular the black working class, were in the city. So the businessmen incited them to go out on strike, paid them to do it! They actually closed up their factory doors and told their workers to go out and strike! And the CIA had also, by this time, penetrated the trade unions and taken root in the Guyana TUC. All this was being whipped up by the Guyanese press at the orders of its owners. Much of this period of our history is documented in my book, *The West on Trial*.

SEARLE: *These are examples of a very overt and vulgar kind of destabilization. Perhaps such methods would not work so easily now with governments like the People's Revolutionary Government of Grenada, which has the hindsight of the experiences of Guyana, Chile and Jamaica.*

Do you think, that particularly in relation to Grenada, imperialism is developing new and more subtle forms of destabilization?

JAGAN: Imperialism, particularly after Watergate, Chile, Vietnam and the furore following the *Ramparts* exposé, sought to bring American politics to a position where they could introduce a new type of man who could restore 'morality' to America. So Nixon was discarded and Carter was brought out of virtual obscurity to head the government, and he began to talk about 'Human Rights' — making this his main line of propaganda. This method, of course, was directed towards the socialist countries, as if there were no 'human rights' there. Then they set up a number of bodies who would examine the usual bourgeois-democratic norms, without considering the *content* of democracy or saying what democracy gives to the people. So they changed their tactics, because the Chilean Pinochet model was galling to a lot of people and the crass way in which Ford put it, when he was asked for what reasons did America act in this way, embarrassed many Americans. He said that sometimes 'we had to do things like this'. So that they *had* to move away from that kind of position, because not only was the economy of America in a shambles in that mid-1970s period — balance of trade, balance of payments, devaluation of the dollar — but also the moral prestige. So that the Christian image of a Carter that they put forward, that we are all brothers and that we want to help you, that we are against the dictatorships, that we want the rights of the people to be respected — all this they used as a camouflage for the same old imperialist policies. So they now attacked governments like Cuba and later Grenada on 'human rights' grounds, and if you didn't practise these bourgeois-democratic forms then the weight of their propaganda would be directed against you.

Then we saw, in the case of the Carter Administration, the more subtle treatment and undermining of the Manley Government in Jamaica. They tried to overthrow it in the 1976 elections with violence and intimidation, but fortunately Manley still won. As soon as he won, they changed their tactics. Carter's wife came to Jamaica and hugged Manley, and said they were now great friends. Then Andrew Young came down and said that he wanted to help them. There was a lot of talk about 'ideological pluralism'. This was clearly a new form of destabilization, but more subtle, and finally they roped Manley into the International Monetary Fund. There was a big division in the ruling party. In February 1977 they rejected going in, but in April, in they went, and that decision helped to destabilize the Manley Government. They eventually broke with the IMF, but by that time it was too late, the harm had already been done. So imperialism is more subtle now, it *imposes* economic planning strategies, models like that of Puerto Rico and the magic of free enterprise.

So now the method is really twofold — both the carrot *and* the stick. The carrot, aimed at putting the economy in the direction of ending up in *the debt trap*, and once you end up there, like Manley did, then your independence is bartered away because you have to concede to the terms which they dictate.

But now Reagan has brought politics back to the Dulles era, back to the big stick, Monroe Doctrine approach. Kennedy and Carter tended to move with a reformist model. After Playa Giron, Kennedy brought in the 'Alliance for Progress' as an alternative to the Cuban revolutionary model. But that failed. Then Carter began to revise that same tactic with his 'human rights' smokescreen over the same old capitalist order. So the destabilization techniques are always shifting, it is not a straight course, it is a flexible process that they use. Before, they would deal with regions as a whole, but now their approach is more bi-lateral, to deal with each government individually. The IMF studies and anatomizes each separate economy; it is now America's main means of economic intelligence. Then they would know how to deal with you and select the appropriate method for destabilizing you. They haven't given up the old methods, but from time to time the emphasis shifts. They pull out methods according to their analysis of the situation of each country, having made a *very careful* study through the CIA of all aspects of the life of that country: the economy, the political forces within the country and the habits of the people. Then they strike.

SEARLE:*What do you think is in their mind about Grenada?*

JAGAN: Grenada has to be put into the general context of their Latin-American policy — as stated in the 'Santa Fé Declaration', made by the advisers to Reagan. In this they said that Soviet communism is the great threat to the region, Cuba is the agent of Soviet expansionism, and Nicaragua and Grenada are agents of Cuba and therefore indirectly agents of the Soviet Union. This is the general thesis: firstly the Cubans must be warned to stop giving support to national liberation struggles — which US imperialism calls terrorism. If the warning is not heeded, then tighten the screw! Then finally, if it is *still* not heeded, then they cannot rule out the option of military aggression. This is how they are operating against Cuba, and the same methods will be used against Nicaragua and Grenada too, while at the same time using all those other methods too: trade unions, Church, economic sabotage. The latter method proved very effective in Chile, where they created a scarcity of spare parts, and in Ghana, where they engineered the drop in the price of cocoa — thus putting the economy in trouble, so that the market women, who were previously the biggest supporters of Nkrumah, were dancing in the streets when he was finally overthrown. The economic sabotage destroyed the balance of payments, obliterated the sources of foreign exchange and so there was no money to pay for the imports which the market women were selling. So now Grenada has a similar problem with the prices of its bananas and nutmegs. We know the multinational companies control these prices and they manipulate them as it suits their policies. They also control the economies of certain countries who can refuse to buy these products. So economic aggression is a big factor which imperialism will use against progressive governments like Grenada — and that is the strongest argument for *diversifying* both products *and* markets.

This is why it is so important for the leadership to be united and constantly with the people. An ideological struggle must be constantly waged and the consciousness of the people continually raised, so that they understand all the wiles and tricks of imperialism. This was one of our problems in Guyana during the 1957–64 period. We had splits in our party in 1955–6 — rightists and ultra-leftists and we were weakened with insufficient cadres. We had so few people to run the party, run the government *and* do ideological work among the masses. And the British were simultaneously working against us all the time. So some sections of the working class, incited by the press and the radio, began to think that we were their enemies. So it is vital *to be with the masses* and do *ideological work*, because once people identify with the Revolution, then they're prepared to make sacrifices — particularly if they see the leadership making sacrifices. Their consciousness must be raised so that they can *understand the causes* of their difficulties, and so their support of the Revolution will remain firm.

SEARLE: *Do you think there are other specific ways in which Grenada can head off destabilization?*

JAGAN: International solidarity — as this conference is showing — is of immense importance. Also it is important to have very close links with the socialist world. Revolution is a totality — when they begin to hit you, you have to have somebody to back you up. Solidarity, aid and trade are all important in this context.

Look at the case of Arbenz. He won an election in Guatemala. He was a military man but relied too much upon the conventional military. So when the CIA-backed invasion took place in 1954, by the time that he gave the guns to the peasants, it was too late! He had no militia, he had not armed the people. Fidel understood Arbenz' failure. He corrected it and armed the people, created a big militia and Committees for the Defence of

the Revolution on every block, just like Grenada has its People's
Revolutionary Militia — that's crucial to preserve the Revolution and Grenada, too, has learned that lesson.

APPENDIX C

From The Free West Indian, *18 October 1980*

'STOP THE GLEANER, AND SAVE LIVES', SAYS PUBLIC ENQUIRY

'Deliberate distortions, unfounded allegations, unwarranted attacks, misleading headlines, definite falsehoods, unsupported accusations, biased reporting, slanted news, inaccurate stories, unbalanced commentaries, and the use of rumours and gossip', summed up the editorial policy of *The Gleaner* Publications, according to a Public Citizens' Inquiry in Jamaica.

The editorial management of *The Gleaner* Publications, the inquiry found, 'appears to have systematically subordinated to narrow interests the ethics of the professional journalist, and even more seriously, the right of the public to truth.' It called upon *The Daily Gleaner*, Jamaica's largest newspaper, and its evening companion, *The Star*, to make a fundamental change towards increased professionalism in their editorial policy and management. Failing this, the inquiry asked those responsible for guiding 'this young nation towards the realization of a balanced dialogue' to 'consider an intervention in the interest of a healing of the desperate wounds from which the country now suffers, as well as, to put it starkly, in the interest of rational security and the saving of thousands of lives.'

The independent inquiry, headed by author and executive director of the Institute of Jamaica, Neville Dawes, included author, journalist and head of the Jamaica National Trust Commission, Vic Reid; the Rev Bevis Byfield of the Jamaica Council of Churches and Dr Peter Figueroa, Medical Officer of Health. The inquiry was set up by the Press Association of Jamaica (PAJ), to enquire into over 150 complaints of unprofessional conduct and violations of the PAJ's Code of Ethics (1965) by *The Gleaner* Publications. The code is to ensure the media serves the collective interests of all the people of the country and affirms and defends human rights and all honest causes. It stresses that the media can only exercise rights, privileges and freedoms, on the understanding that the general public interest and the good of the country is paramount, and where there is conflict between the media's rights and the community's interests, the latter shall prevail.

The inquiry began its thirteen sittings in January and called nineteen witnesses, including former *Gleaner* workers. After studying 200 items of evidence and over 920 written submissions the commissioners found that *The Gleaner* Publications had violated seven of the nine sections of the code. And they found that the 'regulation, frequency and orientation' of many of the violations and the 'marked infrequency of retractions, even where clearly in breach', suggested a conscious editorial policy by the owners.

The most notable witness was American Dr Fred Landis, consultant-researcher to the US Senate Sub-committee on the CIA's covert action in Chile, and author of *Psychological Warfare and Media Operations in Chile, 1970–73*. This is a study of the CIA's use of psychological warfare, through the newspaper *El Mercurio* and its evening companion *La Segunda*, to bring about disorder and the eventual overthrow of President Salvadore Allende.

Psychological warfare, Dr Landis explained, 'is a form of extreme propaganda, ideological terrorism, designed to disorient the population and disintegrate the society to such a level, that the security forces will enter the situation and take over.' Techniques used by *El Mercurio* against Dr Allende's Government, he said, included fabrication of news; misleading juxtaposition of headlines, stories and photographs; correlation of news, editorial and political advertisements; a series of headlines which escalate false charges; use of headlines from other countries and times to further a propaganda theme; and manipulation of subconscious fears. These techniques, are outlined in the *CIA Bi-Weekly Propaganda Guidance* and the *US Army Field Manual of Psychological Warfare*. And he showed the parallel used by the Chilean duo and the *Gleaner* duo. 'The *Gleaner* reflects Chile all over again,' said Dr Landis. 'You only have to study the standardized techniques in one country and you can recognize it anywhere'.

Charges of 'red' and Cuban subversion, the setting up of a Brains Trust, character assassination, emphasis of violence, the call for a military solution, self-promotion and the frequent use of public opinion polls are part of the pattern. *Gleaner* opinion polls are usually conducted by Dr Carl Stone, supporter of the opposition Jamaica Labour Party (JLP), headed by business-man Edward Seaga. Big business money and interests link *The Gleaner* owners, the JLP, the US Government and the Inter-American Press Association (IAPA), which Dr Landis described as 'a rogues' gallery of all the chief executives in the media field for the CIA.' Oliver Clarke, managing director and chairman of *The Gleaner* Publications, is Vice-President of IAPA.

IAPA controls the board which grants the Columbia School of Journalism's Maria Moors Cabot Prize, awarded last year to *The Gleaner* for 'meritorious services'. IAPA's general man-ager, James B Canel, who had a history of associations with the CIA is one of the board's nine directors. Its Director is Arthur Sulzberger, Chairman of *The New York Times* and member of the Council on Foreign Relations, created by Trilateral Com-mission founders David Rockefeller and Zbigniew Brzezinski.

Brzezinski, US National Security Adviser, is a former direc-tor of Columbia's School of International Affairs.

The Gleaner arrogantly refused to take part in the public inquiry, saying that complaints against it should be sent to the Caribbean Press Council (CPC). The commissioners noted that the 'CPC is not known to have any code of ethics of its own'. Moreover, they said, the CPC was established by the Caribbean Publishing and Broadcasting Association (CPBA), an organiza-tion of media managers of which *The Gleaner*'s Clarke is President. CPBA's Chairman is Ken Gordon, managing direc-tor of Trinidad Express Newspapers, a member of IAPA and shareholder in the counter-revolutionary *Torchlight*. The CPBA media bosses recently made an award to *The Torchlight* for what they called 'courageous journalism'.

APPENDIX D

Prime Minister Maurice Bishop's Address to the First Conference of Journalists from the Caribbean Area: St George's, Grenada, April 17th, 1982 (Extracts).

Propaganda Destabilization

I start with the concept of propaganda destabilization. Comrades, the word 'destabilization' is not *our* word, neither is it a concept that belongs to us or a form of behaviour practised by us. You would remember it is a part of the lexicography of the United States Central Intelligence Agency, coined by one of their ex-directors. And yet now it is a word that every Grenadian knows, for our people have known exactly what it means on their pulses and nerves ever since the first dawn of our Revolution. They have experienced destabilization in all its insidious, brutal and most treacherous forms — economic, political, diplomatic and violent destabilization — but its manifestation that has become as much a part of our lives as a bowl of callalloo soup or the scent of nutmegs, is the reality of *propaganda destablization.*

Our people can tune into one of a dozen radio stations and hear reports, purportedly about Grenada, but in truth about a fictional country that has never existed. They can buy newspapers that print such blatant lies and disinformation as to create the screenplay for the most fantastic and vulgar of Hollywood melodramas, notwithstanding the remarkable record ex-Hollywood actors have sometimes seemed to demonstrate in that particular field of endeavour. If they take with any degree of seriousness at all the extraordinary mixture of reports in the regional and North American press about military bases and activity here, then instead of the peaceful, verdant and productive island on which they live, they would behold as their homeland a stark militarized zone of tar and concrete which would appear like an uneasy combination of Pearl Harbor, Chelsea Barracks, Cape Kennedy, West Point and the Panama Canal Zone—with fighter planes as numerous as our butterflies and nuclear submarines in flotillas like shoals of sprats! In fact, the grotesquerie of the propaganda caricature of Grenada has reached such a point of high farce and such levels of hallucination and absurdity as to have completely refuted itself.

However, rejection of the lies of the media mafia is now easy for our people in Grenada as we have set in motion in our country a profound level of mass mobilization and mass education—which we believe to be twin aspects of the same process— that has made our people constantly vigilant and concerned to unravel, understand and defend the *truth* of events. We have said before that we hold the truth itself to be revolutionary and we shall stand firm by its side. Propaganda destabilization and the systematic manipulation of falsehood, as practised by journalists unworthy of the name and media interests who have only corruption and decadence to defend, is perhaps the most sophisticated form of lying that human society — or perhaps it would be more accurate to say *anti*-human society — has ever generated. We have witnessed examples of this grisly phenomenon over the last few years in our continent, perpetrated and orchestrated by the CIA, that would out-goebbels Goebbels, that most monstrous purveyor of the lie. But the unleashed force of an organized people, a conscious people, a vigilant people, a united people, a people who are educating themselves and each other through their political process, a people who are stopping not only to *listen*, but also to analyze, criticise and discuss everything in their country from the budget to calypsoes to public health to events in El Salvador, Namibia or the Western Sahara, cannot be deceived or fooled so easily. They stand as interpreters *and* protectors of the truth. In the same way that they patrol and guard the beaches of our country from physical attack, they are also guardians of the truth. In the same way that they are training themselves to repel any mercenary or imperialist incursion, they are also, through an accompanying process, training themselves to dispel the lies and slander that insult the truth of their progress and distort their Revolution.

But although imperialist propaganda destabilization has out-lied and out-libelled itself and exposed its own rotting carcase in the process, honest and dedicated journalists clearly have a huge responsibility and obligation to hasten its final and inevitable self-destruction, for it has caused enormous and blood-soaked damage throughout its rabid lifespan, and continues to do so in its throes of death. In Grenada we have carefully analyzed the extent of its devastation in Chile and Jamaica through such newspapers as *El Mercurio* and the *Daily Gleaner* respectively, and knowing what was set loose there, nothing the imperialist press can invent and say about us can ever give us any surprises. We have read page after page of lies about us, ingeniously concocted by the hirelings of some of the richest media merchants in the world — about *us*, whose population would only amount to heads counted in a small North American city! *The Boston Globe, The Washington Post, The New York Times, The Christian Science Monitor, The Miami Herald, The Wall Street Journal, The Los Angeles Times, Newsweek, Time* — why should they spend so much time, labour and printer's ink writing about our tiny nation and composing more and more fantasy abour our process?

In West Germany, shortly after our Revolution, *Bunte* Magazine told us that we had a lightning-erected Soviet missile base, with warheads aimed at neighbouring islands, perched somewhere like a fairy castle on the rugged peaks around the Grand Etang which you would have passed when you crossed over the central ridge of our island on your way from Pearls' Airport to St George's. Then, after a long, taxing and strenuous campaign to raise money to pay for our New International Airport which will have *one* 9,000 foot runway, the British Broadcasting Corporation obligingly informs us that in fact we are putting down *three* runways, thus wishing that exhausting process on us again twice-over! Indeed, with the recent reports in the London *Daily Telegraph* of yet another secret submarine base at Calivigny on our South-East coast, you might be excused for blinking your eyes and for a moment *not* believing you are in the National Conference Centre of Free Grenada but on a Hollywood film studio watching the filming of one of those old Z rated movies that Ronald Reagan used to enjoy acting in so much in his younger days. However, the extraordinary reality is, that while these fantastic stories circulate unashamedly in the imperialist press, and make out our beloved island to be a sinister haven of international intrigue, our people still work and produce in their gardens, factories and farms; our tourists enjoy our beaches and waterfalls and go for rides in mini-mokes all over our island; six hundred American medical students continue to apply themselves seriously to their studies, and our people in their busloads take Sunday afternoon excursions, having picnics, collect shells thrown up by the dredge at Hardy Bay and fly their kites with happiness and pride over their international airport project which they recognize correctly as the most important and vital economic project that our country has ever undertaken.

Comrades, we know that the CIA has direct access to over 200 newspapers. We also know that it puts out its *Bi-weekly Propaganda Guidance* to radio stations right through our continent. We know of the twisted techniques it uses to control those conservative newspapers in 'flashpoint' countries it needs to destabilize progressive governments. We know how the newspaper editors and owners concerned are promoted overnight to the Board of Directors of the Inter-American Press Association at the outset of this destabilizing process, for the sake of artificially boosting the prestige of their rags. We have observed this clearly again in the case of *El Mercurio* in Chile, and more recently, in the case of Oliver Clarke, the publisher of the Jamaica *Daily Gleaner*. We have noted the way in which progressive typesetters and designers on these target newspapers have been summarily dismissed and replaced by misguided elements, who, by using word-association techniques, pictorial insinuation, emotive symbolism and the juxtaposition of negative images with photographs of progressive leaders, have attempted to spread disorder, demoralization, distrust and fear amongst the readership of these journals.

We also know how the editors of the largest and wealthiest newspapers in the Caribbean were invited to Washington in May, 1981 by the United States International Communications Agency, (USICA), the propaganda arm of the US State Department, for a crash course in these honourable professional techniques, and how a few weeks later the ignoble concept of the Free Press under imperialism was further dignified with identical front page editorials pouring ridiculous but sordid lie after lie, comma for comma, full stop for full stop on Grenada in the columns of *The Gleaner*, *The Barbados Sunday Sun*, the *Barbados Advocate*, the *Trinidad Guardian* and the *Trinidad*

Express. In this we saw the clumsy and unethical hypocrisy and dishonesty practised by the Caribbean proxies of the major US press goliaths. Their lack of deftness clearly shows that they still have a lot to learn from their USICA masters and teachers, and we can confidently expect a return seminar for a little remedial education for Mr Gordon, Mr Wynter, Mr Clarke and their backward classmates.

USICA and IAPA — Twin Enemies of Democratic Journalism

Perhaps at this point it would be instructive for us to consider USICA and IAPA a little more closely. USICA was born from its mother organization, the United States Information Agency (USIA). The Deputy Director of this illustrious organization, one Thomas C. Sorenson, said in the 1960's that: 'The USIA is the psychological instrument of the US Government overseas, just as the State Department is the diplomatic instrument of the Agency for International Development, (USAID) the economic assistance instrument, and the Central Intelligence Agency, (CIA) the intelligence instrument.' And as you can see this is quite a constellation, comrades! So let there be no doubts as to the motives of the USICA seminar for the Caribbean media-chiefs. For this 'psychological instrument' is openly waging war on the minds of the Caribbean and Latin American masses, taking many leaves from the US Army's *Field Manual on Psychological Warfare*. In what is perhaps the zenith of cynicism, this enlightened document, required reading for all propaganda destabilizers, says quite bluntly:

'Peace . . . is the continuation of war by non-military means.

Psychological activities are those carried out in peace time, or in places other than war theatres, in order to influence the feelings, attitudes and foreign groups in a manner favourable to the achievement of the policies of the United States.'

And even though many of our Caribbean editors and newspaper owners went running to their master's voice in Washington bursting with enthusiasm, it is important to remember that the 'country team' in any US Embassy will contain not only military attaches, a CIA station chief, USAID heads and a Peace Corps co-ordinator — but also the head of the local USICA mission, who is aiming his psychological arrows constantly at

the political and economic power structures, trade union leaders, opposition prospects, editors, broadcasters, educators,
community leaders and anyone else likely to serve his ends.

USICA's grim twin is IAPA, whom we met earlier as the
kindly sponsor of the destabilization blitz in Chile and Jamaica.
This organization, which has a truly impressive record of
orchestration of outright slander, lies and scurrilous calumny
was again the progeny of the US State Department from whence
all good and pure destabilizing instruments come. It was first
formed in 1926 as the *First Pan-American Congress of Journalists*, and seized in 1950 by the CIA after it had passed to the
leadership of a group of independent-minded journalists — a
state of affairs, or course, intolerable to US State structures.
Since then it has singlemindedly dedicated itself to a crusade
against truth, and has been decorated many times for its intrepid
attacks upon journalistic honesty and integrity.

Comrades, Grenada is a free area which is liberating itself
from the false perspectives and distorting moulds of imperialism. Our people are developing the critical consciousness and
powers of discrimination to detect propaganda destabilization
whenever and however it threatens them. It is a strange contrad-
iction that the attempts at destabilization hurled against our
country by newspaper and radio are themselves *steeling our
people* and sharpening their critical sense, making them more
able and committed to identify, resist and beat back the lies.
Every slander thrown at us presents a mental manoeuvre for our
people, an exercise which strengthens their consciousness and
mind muscles. In this sense, the propaganda destabilizers are
unwittingly doing our people a favour, for they are creating
within the minds of our people a determined mental militia
which launches back a hundredfold of truth for every single
falsehood aimed at our country. Having lived through an
apprenticeship of lies daily striking our shores, our people are
building the fabric of resolution and truth which they are
offering to the world. For here in Grenada, *falsehood shall not
pass*, even though it is the daily bread of imperialism.

Democracy and the Caribbean Press

Comrades, in order to seriously consider democracy and the
press, we need to examine the situation in which the majority of

Caribbean journalists apparently find themselves locked. The working journalist is a true producer. He follows and hunts the news, he hustles for stories, he uncovers the submerged truth of events, he blasts open secrets and corruption with his investigative dynamite. Alongside his colleagues who produce and print the newspaper, he is the *worker of news*. And yet his product is not his. His work is valued solely in terms of how he contributes towards making profits for the owner of his medium, which is a commodity to be bought and sold at a market place like a pound of salt-fish or a pile of mangoes. While he strikes out towards the truth, the owner of his words and columns counts up his dollars and looks for ways of making more. And if prostituting the truth is the way forward towards that end, then so be it!

So how then, does the honest journalist, whose work is alienated, relegated and despised, act? We have seen some courageous resistance in relation to our own country, when the calculated and co-ordinated swapping of falsehoods and vitriolic anti-Grenada editorials launched through a corrupt section of the Caribbean Press by the United States International Communications Agency, (USICA), was met with a determined and principled act of protest by some of your Trinidadian colleagues, but many other regional journalists would prefer to work on in their own way, in their own individual niche, and continue to interpret that existence as 'the freedom of the press', even though their stories are cut or warped, even though their opinion in the enterprise in which they work is counted for nothing, even though they have no control over their working conditions, even though they have no say in the political direction of their newspaper, even though their just wage demands are treated with the same scorn as their skills and opinions, even though the decisions affecting their newspaper are taken over the clinking of glasses filled with *Chivas Regal Scotch* at a luxurious country club. While the true journalist works with the people, searching out the truth of their lives and problems and writing stories seeking to expose the conditions bearing down on their hope for progress, their employers machinate with the forces of falsehood, the media-monsters of the CIA and Inter-American Press Association, the anti-people, anti-progress robots and psychopaths who are completely and unscrupulously machiavellian in their appetite to distort all reality and shape it in the moulds of the voracious multi-national corporations.

These are the forces who claim to have sanctified the principles of Press Freedom, who control the region's editorials, who prefer to print the computerised calumny of 'top Pentagon officials' to the real views and naked words of the Caribbean people.

Let us take for example the *Trindiad Guardian* of Wednesday 3 March of this year. You would have seen the elegant headline emblazoned across the front page with the original, well-chosen words, *Grenada Base Open to Reds*, where one American Fred, (Fred S. Hoffman) a journalist, quotes another American Fred (Dr Fred C. Ikle) a US Undersecretary of Defence, with more unsubstantiated lies and slander about how our International Airport is to become 'an airbase available to the Soviet Union'. If the hard-working Caribbean journalist or the bemused Caribbean reader begins to scratch his head in bewilderment at where *his own people, his own aspirations, his own country* begins to fit into this network of Freds and international scandal, it would not be unreasonable. His own land, his own issues, his own problems have been leap-frogged, set aside and deemed irrelevant. His voice is nothing, the screaming and shrieking of the US State Department is clearly more important to the *Trinidad Guardian* than his Caribbean existence. And yet this so-called 'democratic press' always seeking, as it so often tells us, to present all sides of the story, in the case of the March 3 article, as indeed many other articles *refused to print* the letter of response sent by the People's Revolutionary Government two days later, and up until now, has not even had the democratic manners to sent back an acknowledgement.

We in Grenada were not surprised at these proceedings, neither have we been surprised at the dozens of other similar outpourings of lies and garbage which characterize the columns of the *Trinidad Guardian* or the *Trinidad Express*. This is not to say that we are not also continually disgusted at the growing intensity and desperation of these utterances, but we have made our customary analysis of those who seek to defame us, and we understand their motives, for we understand the real power behind these pages. These papers which proudly boast their independence, in fact speak with the same voice and the interests of the same class. Jointly, there are eighteen directors on the boards of those two newspapers. Of the ten about whom information exists, they have interlocking directorships in 47 other companies, including national, regional and multinational business corporations such as insurance and stock-broking companies and several banks, namely the Bank of Commerce, the Royal Bank of Canada, Barclays and the locally-owned National Commercial. Clearly, journalistic integrity and democratic aspirations do not go hand-in-hand with such interests, and should the journalist of such enterprises wonder who he is truly serving, the facts are there before him.

Is it surprising that such forces would attack, with so much bile and bitterness, the advances of the Grenada Revolution? Is it surprising that the knowledge of a proud and free people in an island just across the sea, who are emancipating their muscles and intellects, who are claiming their right to control and direct their own destiny, build their own economy and cast away tyranny into the furthest memory of history, should provoke such passionate and maniacal fear among these paper barons? A poor people gaining wealth through participation and organiza-tion, a people casting their own moulds, a people resolved to finish with mimicry and fear. No wonder they are frightened, for the spectre that haunts their drunken nights, the image which dances at the bottom of their Martini glasses, the shiver that shakes their flesh in their air-conditioned offices is the vision of the free people of Grenada building a new life on the ruins and wreckage of the system they uphold, and the terrible thought that the readers of their own newspapers will one day, sooner than they fear, boldly take a parallel road.

This is why these newspapers whilst printing millions of words of lies about our process have printed nothing about our new revolutionary grassroots democracy here in Grenada, and why you will read pitifully few lines about our mass organiza-tions, our Workers' Parish Councils, our Zonal Councils. And you will find next to nothing about these remarkable and vibrant structures of our people's power — our organs of popular democracy in other newspapers up and down the region that are owned and managed by the same parasitical cabal. Ken Gordon, for example, of the *Trinidad Express*, is also a transnational media magnate, with a part ownership in the *St Lucia Voice*, the *Barbados Nation,* and the late, but not lamented *Torchlight*, which he used as a base of slanderous and destabilizing opera-tions here in Grenada.

Because we do not fear the lies of the imperialists and their proxies, we allow into our country *every day* their newspapers and magazines with all their distortions against us. Any day on the streets and in newspaper shops of our country, you can buy the 'Trinidad Express', the 'Trinidad Guardian', 'The Bomb', 'Challenge', 'Target', the 'Barbados Advocate', 'Time' or 'Newsweek' magazine but every week, notwithstanding our best efforts, you cannot buy on their streets our national newspaper 'The Free West Indian'. Yet, they are the ones who speak of press freedom.

I want to give you the benefit of some research done by our Media Workers Association. They analyzed the 19 month period from June 1980 to December 1981; to be more concrete they did a content analysis of a section of Caribbean press coverage during that period for the following newspapers 'Trinidad Guardian', 'Trinidad Express', 'Vincentian', 'Voice of St Lucia', 'Dominica Chronicle', 'Barbados Advocate', 'Barbados Nation' and occasional copies of the 'Jamaica Gleaner' and the 'Trinidad Bomb' newspapers. What this analysis showed is that during this 19 month period, these papers carried some 1570 articles on Grenada and our Revolution, which works out to an average of nearly 3 articles per day. Some 60 per cent of these were editorial or other comment and the remaining 40 per cent was 'straight' news. About 60 per cent of these articles were negative towards the Grenada Revolution being either downright lies or subtle and not so subtle distortions. Furthermore, 95 per cent of the PRG's rebuttals to many of these scandalous and libellous articles were never published.

It is clear that no other topic has attracted such vast coverage in this section of the Caribbean press over the last 3 years. And Comrades will, of course, note that only some newspapers in a handful of islands are included without reference to radio or television coverage and also that the vast press and other media coverage in the rest of the Caribbean, Latin America, North America and Western Europe is excluded altogether from this analysis. There is no doubt that the Grenada Revolution has been very profitable for the media magnates and salt-fish mafia of the region.

So what do we in Grenada raise in the place of the great democratic sham of the imperialist press? Where do we seek the forms of our press democracy? We uphold the freedom of the majority of the working people, who form the mass of our population, to express their views and their right to have access to the mass media which serves their interests, which reflects their struggles and aspirations, their perceptions and opinions.

We vindicate a media which is a tool to help organize and mobilize our people, for without that constant activity and participation there is no democracy, no collective strength. We add that our media must inform our people honestly and seek to educate them, it must provide them with constructive criticism for the examination of problems and the formulation of solutions, with the opportunity to advance proposals and ideas that will help to form the country's domestic and foreign policies. As such, it is crucial that the people's letters and complaints are openly printed for public comment, and conversely in the spirit of the principles of Emulation, that the most outstanding of our workers receive appreciation and recognition through our newspapers, radio and television. To implement these principles, there are 9 regular newspapers published in Grenada, in place of the only one rag that was being printed before the Revolution. And a new newspaper, *Fedon*, the voice of the People's Revolutionary Armed Forces is to begin publication in the next few days. Their owners are the masses and their mass organizations. Look and scan with every means you have, comrades, you will find no directors of foreign banks editing or managing *The Free West Indian, Women's Voice, Fight, The New Jewel, The Pioneers Voice, Cutlass, Fork, Media Workers Voice,* or the *Workers Voice*. There is a newspaper serving all the major elements of our society: our youth, our women, our trade unionists, and our children, as well as our national newspaper, *The Free West Indian,* which binds these constituent parts together.

Comrades, we cannot tell you, neither would we presume to tell you, to duplicate our experience here in Grenada, in your own countries. Your means of democratizing your media will arise out of your *own* conditions, your *own* struggles, your *own* definitions. But every inch of ground gained in your workplaces is a liberated area for the entire Caribbean, every assault upon organized lying is a blow for truth which benefits every working person of the Caribbean, every defeat of the press barons in things great and small means a few steps forward for all our people. Words *are* weapons, and the vested interests of the Caribbean media are pointing them not only at us in Grenada, but at any oppressed or scrunting group that begin to stand up for a new and better life. Comrades, we must *turn the words around*, aim them back at the exploiters and begin to free our Caribbean Journalism of the despair and tyranny which holds it in a vice, and permits no democratic advance. You are the writers, you hold the weapons. You have the power to create your own notions and structures of Press Freedom that will expose and obliterate the terrible untruths that have made it, in the mouths of the ruling class of the Press, the greatest and hollowest falsity of our age.

Journalism and the Struggle for Peace

Comrades, although there may be differences between us in some matters, there is one issue in particular upon which, above all, I am certain that we stand absolutely united. I am referring to the question of *Peace*, and the common commitment that we share to make our region a *zone of peace*. Perhaps such an assertion has even greater significance at this present time, when the forces of the North Atlantic Treaty Organisation, led by the hawks of the United States of America, are preparing once more to turn our Caribbean Sea into an armed lake. Like an over-grown child at his bathtime, President Reagan is about to drop into what he believes is his bathtub, his fleet of toy battleships and aircraft carriers filled to the brim with plastic planes and clockwork marines. I speak, of course, to the soon-to-be-realized military manoeuvres code-named *Ocean Venture 82*, which are shortly to strike our region.

Such huge military rehearsals, so perilously close to our shores, and in fact *including* the shores of our comrades in Cuba and the occupied earth of Puerto Rico, only demonstrate one more time the proximity of war and the blasé, imperial and Monroe doctrine-like attitude of the United States to our region and waters. The impunity with which their carriers of war float around our Caribbean is only encouraged by those governments which say that a shipload of American sailors in port bringing in thousands of dollars to their foreign exchange justifies their presence in our seas. Let us be clear that such money is nothing more than the wages of war, the cost of prostituting our sisters, the mercenary price paid to harass and threaten our region, to militarize it and turn it into a potential theatre of war and as such it can never be justified!

In this context, it is crucial that our regional journalists accomplish their sacred mission to be the propagandists of peace. Mere sabre-rattling has developed into the rumbling of aircraft carriers and the hissing of nuclear missiles, and these are the noises we shall be hearing more and more in our region while the present US warmongering continues. Any journalist that seeks to preserve peace and help to secure a future for humanity has a decisive role and responsibility *here* and *now*, that of monitoring the warlords, keeping on their tail, never losing sight of them, constantly supplying detailed and exact information on their movements and violations, and keeping continually vigilant to their threats and provocations.

In our own region we have had a particularly admirable example of such investigative power by some of our journalists. For years in two islands of the Caribbean, Antigua and Barbados, a transnational munitions company was secretly developing and testing a lethal artillery device on behalf of the South African racist government. This giant howitzer was not only used to lob and explode a nuclear warhead some five miles into the upper atmosphere, but also to shell and murder our African comrades in Angola during the abortive South African invasion into that sovereign state while the brave Angolans were fighting their Second War of Liberation. The foul and clandestine work of this transnational company, which operated under bogus respectability as the *Space Research Corporation*, was unmasked by courageous and outstanding journalists both in Barbados and Antigua. Their probing work had important consequences, for it resulted in this poisonous company being ejected from both islands. As such, it was a blow not only for the preservation of peace in our region and an expulsion of the racist scientists of death, but also a victory on behalf of the oppressed and struggling people of South Africa, for every deprivation of weaponry the Pretoria regime suffers, gives more hope and inspiration to the South African liberation forces and brings their inevitable victory a step forward. It must be emphasized that our quest for peace here in the Caribbean and the exposing of warmongering and bellicose initiatives provoked by imperialism in our *own* region by our *own* journalists, is not only good for our own dignity; but has a global significance, for in the age of thermonuclear arms the threat to peace even in a speck of the world like two very small islands barely seen on a world map is a threat to peace for the entire world.

In this epoch, comrades, the eyes of the world are staring squarely at our region. They see our Caribbean as a flashpoint, a trouble spot, with an intensity that we have never experienced before. The struggle of our heroic neighbours, first in Nicaragua and now in El Salvador and Guatemala, has made our region the world's focus, the target for international journalism. The future of humanity is being fought out on our doorstep, and the need for accurate, pro-human, democratic and progressive journalism in such a scenario is unprecedented in our region. The integrity of Caribbean journalism has never been so necessary, so fundamental, so critical as it is now. The warmongers and tyrants know well that the honest journalist, no matter what his personal ideology may be, is an obvious and natural ally of the national liberation movement. He is recording resistance to oppression, the struggle for bread and justice, the hope and aspiration towards a better life. Whether it was Herbert Matthews, an American, covering the struggle of Fidel and his comrades in the Sierra Maestra, Wilfred Burchett's reporting from Vietnam, the dispatches and articles by Basil Davidson from the liberated zones of Guinea-Bissau, Angola and Mozambique, or John Reed's inspiring words from revolutionary Russia in 1917, the journalist is the crucial link between the fighter for freedom and peace and the man or woman reading a newspaper in any street in any city or village in any country.

This is plainly why the ex-five star general of the defeated US Army in Vietnam, General Westmoreland, is now openly declaring that in any future conflict involving the United States, the American and International press must be restricted, and must not have open access to the battle zones. He knows, perhaps better than anyone, how much American public opinion was turned against the US Vietnamese adventure through the day-by-day reporting from the front line by newspaper, radio and television, and how the American people grew sickened, appalled and ashamed by the vile brutal actions of their own soldiers, by the defoliation and chemical warfare. Westmoreland and others of his ilk understand only too well how American parents — many of them poor — were watching with increasing horror the futile maiming and permanent destruction of their own sons on the television screen while standing in their own living rooms, or how ordinary Americans who talked glibly about the great American dream sat transfixed as they watched the newsreels showing the cold-blooded torture and execution of young men who were supposed to be Viet Cong suspects. Clearly, after that war, journalism could never be the same again, and nothing did more to resolutely change American public opinion and put it against the war, despite the continued frothings and splutterings of the warlords.

In the same way, in June 1979 in Nicaragua, when the American public saw a news film of the arbitrary and merciless killing of an ABC correspondent by one of Somoza's National Guard, there was a horrified and incredulous outcry through America which quite clearly made it extremely difficult for the US hawks to take the option they wanted of direct military intervention in Nicaragua. Thus this event was to prove very significant for the eventual Sandinista victory. And we could compare a situation, as in Nicaragua or El Salvador, where the press are able to cover the war, despite the immense difficulties, to a situation where they cannot. In East Timor, the FRETILIN soldiers of national liberation have been waging a six-year war with irrepressible courage, against the Indonesian armed forces, who invaded their country a week after it achieved its independence following centuries of Portuguese Colonialism in 1976. East Timor, an enclave on an island in South East Asia, has been sealed off from journalists by an air and sea blockade, and receives scant publicity and little reporting. Consequently, the just struggle of its people has never received the kind of international solidarity of other struggles for peace and justice that have been more prolifically covered by international journalism. The result is that a heroic people continue a massive struggle in virtual isolation, and carry forward their drive towards freedom under a serious disadvantage — a vacuum of press coverage.

So comrades, in this present period, when national liberation struggles and the demands of the poor and working people dominate our region and much of the world, it is the right *and* responsibility of the journalist of integrity to move to cover them, to report upon them, to photograph, film and record them, to spread out the news of their people's struggles from Namibia, from El Salvador, from South Africa, from East Timor, from the Western Sahara, from Palestine. For their cause and the cause of all oppressed and struggling peoples march side by side with the cause of peace. There can be no true peace while the lives of these heroic people with justice on their side are dominated by tyranny or circumscribed by oppression.

Our times are full and echoing with the insane talk of war. In the United States there is the attempt by the disciples of the monstrous industrial–military complex to legitimize the concepts of 'limited nuclear war', the 'First Strike' option, the dangerous concept of 'linkage', the Reagan Doctrine of total uncritical support for international outlaw regimes like Zionist Israel and racist South Africa because they best represent the global expansionist and warlike ambitions of the neutron warlords. Many journalists are falling into the fatal trap of favorably publicising, and thus giving credence to this madness. Clearly, freedom-loving and peace-loving journalists must take the firmest possible stand against such jockeying with the future of our earth, our humanity and everything our people have ever wrested from their history and everything we have ever built for our children. On this fundamental question of peace, disarmament, detente and peaceful co-existence, we must stand united and nothing must tear us apart, for over and above everything else it stands as the most vital issue of our day, the first issue and the last issue: the right to life itself, for any and all of our peoples.

Journalists Must Promote the Cause of Peace

Faced with this historic responsibility, comrades, how can progressive journalists counter such vile propaganda designed to whip up fear and hysteria and create an artificial and erroneous public opinion among the people of our Americas? How can they exercise their responsibility to the ideals for peace and disarmament shared by a growing majority of mankind?

We wish to suggest a number of ways that democratic and progressive journalists using their pens and microphones can wage ideological struggle against the forces of reaction, misinformation and mystification.

Tell your readers and your listeners that peaceful coexistence is a necessity, indeed, that there is no alternative to world peace, that detente is advantageous to all countries, that the right to live in peace is the most basic human right, the guarantor of all other rights.

Explain to your readers and your listeners that the objective of international relations should be disarmament, not arms races and show them how the collossal amount of resources now being squandered on arms should be used to solve the great universal problems of hunger, poor health, illiteracy, substandard housing etc.

Expose to your readers and your listeners that the drift towards war and military intervention is not in the interest of the peoples of our Americas but only serves the military–industrial–state complex's greed for ever greater profits from the manufacture and sale of weapons.

Highlight in your news reports and commentaries all proposals for disarmament, all disarmament conferences, the activities of the growing peace movement around the world and the efforts to have the Caribbean declared and recognized in practice as a Zone of Peace.

Expose in your papers and on your radio and television stations the lies against the Cuban Revolution, the Nicaraguan Revolution, the Surinamese process, the Grenadian Revolution and the truth and reality of the reasons for the struggles of the oppressed peoples of El Salvador, Guatemala and elsewhere.

We in Grenada believe that the peoples of the world have the fundamental right to obtain an objective idea of reality with the help of clear and precise information and at the same time the right to freely express their opinion through the mass media.

The Emperor Visits the Region

Comrades, I wish to take this opportunity to restate Grenada's views on the one news event which has surpassed all others in recent times in the coverage it received from the Caribbean mass media — President Reagan's visit to our region last week.

The character of this visit and the inflammatory remarks made by President Reagan constituted a fundamental insult to the people of Barbados, the people of the Caribbean and the regional journalist community.

Firstly, Reagan ignores Mr Michael Manley, opposition leader in Jamaica during his one day visit there, then shortly after landing in Barbados, on the soil of a sister Caricom nation, he launches a vehement attack on Grenada, another member of the Caribbean Community.

During his four-day stay he insultingly refuses to drive in a car provided by the Barbadian people, or eat Barbadian food or accept the quality of Barbadian health care. This illustrious gentleman who fancies himself as a 20th century Emperor not only takes with him a royal entourage of hundreds of courtiers and minions armed even with their own toilet paper but also a battalion of swarming Western newsmen who enjoy free access to all the places and events that the Emperor graces with his presence, while Barbadian and Caribbean journalists are harassed, bullied and denied their national and professional rights to cover the visit by Reagan's crew of racist security goons.

This insult, this imperial arrogance, this wanton and contemptible disrespect on the sovereign soil of our region, comrades, deserves the strongest condemnation from all democratic and independent minded people of *our* Caribbean.

And there are lessons that Caribbean journalists and Caribbean Journalism must glean from such experiences, for what we witnessed last week are the characteristics of an insensitive millionaire who represents the interests of an imperialistic ruling class whose so-called concern for the region's people is crassly opportunistic. Caribbean journalism therefore cannot set itself apart in some illusionary ivory tower of objectivity and not raise its voice against this and similar abuses, insults and disrespectful and imperialist practices against the independent, sovereign and freedom-loving people of *our* region. No. Indeed Caribbean journalism has the duty and responsibility to side with exploited and oppressed masses of *our* region against monopoly control.

For as long as there are social classes in our societies, and as long as our region and the world is divided into rich and poor, haves and have nots, privileged and under-privileged journalism cannot exist and function outside of these contradictions.

It cannot be independent of society, it cannot be uncommitted to topical social problems because it would lose its purpose and cease to be journalism at all. On the contrary, only in its close connection with society, with the forces of progress or the forces of backwardness do we find the substance and purpose of journalism's existence.